Bonding Tips for Building Loving Relationships

Though I have 37 years of experience as an educator, and a doctorate, my 28 years as a mother and 6 years as a grandmother have taught me more about life than anything I have studied. Where was this book when I was teaching "Growth and Human Development?"

Michael Ray King's book, *Fatherhood 101—Bonding Tips for Building Loving Relationships*, is a quick read that will prove valuable to grandparents, as well as new parents. Whether grandparents live close or far from their new grandchildren, this book serves as a quiet reminder of the higher levels of learning about life and family.

Fatherhood 101—Bonding Tips for Building Loving Relationships will be a good addition to the class reading list for students of education and psychology and definitely would be a nice coffee table book in waiting rooms of doctors, whether pediatricians or obstetricians.

Dr. Cassandra Bolyard Whyte, EdD, Vice President of Administrative Services for West Virginia State University…37 years of experience in higher education as an administrator and teacher

Mr. King has done a wonderful job of putting good parenting advice in a fun, easy reading format. His tips and recommendations would be a priceless gift to not only new fathers, but the wives/partners of those fathers as well. Every American household with children should have a copy of this insightful book.

Tammy Coates, MS, CRC Vocational Case Manager, Carolina Case Management and Rehabilitation Services

Michael King has taken a difficult time in any father's life, whether this be his first child or his fifth, and has placed it in terms all fathers can understand. *Fatherhood 101: Bonding Tips for Building Loving Relationships* was easy to read and also enjoyable. He has also noted an important time in a baby's life, and that is before the baby is born. I feel that by following Mr. King's advice, you will have a more enjoyable and fulfilling time with your children in the first year of their lives. This is an important time to build the strong bonds that will last forever.

Robert E. Dupree, Jr. MD, FACOG
(Fellow American College of Obstetrics & Gynecology)

Michael King knows babies, and is willing to share what he knows with the ones who need it the most: new dads! This easy-to-follow book takes the novice through the baby steps the new dad needs to take successfully on his adventurous path into fatherhood and a healthy, happy relationship with baby.

Kimberly Queen Moldt, MA, NCC, LMHC, LMFT, LPC
(National Certified Counselor, Licensed Mental Health Counselor and Licensed Marriage and Family Therapist in Florida, Licensed Professional Counselor in West Virginia)

Fatherhood 101: Bonding Tips for Building Loving Relationships is a refreshing and practical book. Bonding with your newborn is such an important subject. Michael King covers it well in a clear, practical, and readable book, "*Fatherhood 101.*" As a pastor with a strong background in psychology and counseling, I can heartily recommend this book. The importance of the principles covered here cannot be overstated. For anyone expecting to become a father, or anyone who is a father, I would call this a MUST READ. Any parent, grandparent or foster parent could benefit greatly from reading it.

David A. Bush, BA (Sociology and Psychology), MA (Psychology), MDiv (Master of Divinity)

This is a great read for new fathers who are taking fatherhood and the responsibilities of parenting very seriously. Lots of good information!

Jill deVries, RN, Certified Nurse Life Care Planner, Medicare Set Aside Consultant/ Certified

This book is a straightforward reminder of the importance of fathers in the lives of their children and an encouragement to fathers to step up and make the time to be involved, whether you are having your first child, or your ninth.

Paul J. Waddle, Child Welfare Program Administrator, Social Worker for 20 years, father of five, grandfather of one

Michael King's work touches the heart, the head, and the spirit of raising children. Chock full of humorous anecdotes and illustrations, the author reaches in to touch the essence of being a dad. Don't miss this tender, delightful, personal adventure in the experiences of male parenting!

The Reverend Dr. Steven R. Thomas, Jr.
Pastor, First Presbyterian Church, Cazenovia, New York

Michael King has written a nice book on a topic with which he has both familiarity and experience. I really enjoyed reading this book, and found it interesting and easy to understand. I like the way Mr. King continuously mentions mom and helping mom.

Kimberly Bailey, RN

Fatherhood 101:

Bonding Tips for Building Loving Relationships

Michael Ray King

ClearView Press, Inc., Palm Coast, FL

Fatherhood 101: Bonding Tips for Building Loving Relationships
Copyright © 2008 by ClearView Press, Inc.
Cover Design and photos by Rik Feeney. All rights reserved.
Artwork design by Kim Kunkel. All rights reserved.
Book Coach Rik Feeney
Content Editor Tom Wallace
Copy Editors Diane Legg, Helen King, and Rik Feeney

King, Michael Ray, 1958—
        Fatherhood 101: Bonding Tips for Building Loving Relationships
        124 p. ill. cm.
        ISBN 0-9799623-1-8 (hc)   ISBN 0-9799623-0-1 (sc)
        1. Parenting—Fatherhood—Relationships. I. Title.
HQ756
649.1   LCCN 2008922137

ClearView Press, Inc.
PO Box 353431
Palm Coast, FL 32135-3431
www.clearviewpress.net

Printed in the United States of America

This book is dedicated to my six wonderful children without whom I would be totally lost, and most of all my incredible wife, Bobbie, who is always there to support me in anything I endeavor to accomplish.

Contents

ACKNOWLEDGMENTS

My deepest thanks to my book coach, Rik Feeney, for his invaluable help (and patience), my two writers' groups——The Professional Writers of St. Augustine and the Legare Gang——for their support and feedback, and my best friend and editor, Diane Legg, for her support and input.

My content editor, Tom Wallace, took the pain out of editing and made it an enjoyable and enlightening experience for which I am truly thankful.

I am very grateful for my father, Robert L. King. Many of the most wonderful attributes of the passion to be a writer, I can see in his personality. God blessed me with a very creative father.

My mother, Helen Drake King, inspired me with the publication of her book – *Yesterday's Diary* – and her unwavering support of my authorial efforts. Again, blessed by her creativity as well, there is no doubt in my mind that my desire to write comes naturally.

Introduction

This book is about bonding techniques for new fathers. A new baby creates a *new father*, even if this is his sixth child. Each of my children presented a new personality, a new set of challenges and arrived at different stages of my own growth and maturity. I handle certain things better now than I did with my first few children, but as I'm learning with my three-week-old daughter, I still need some help.

So, if you're expecting a child, know that you'll soon qualify as a *new father*. I'm convinced that even if I fathered fifteen children (Bobbie, please ignore that!), I would still have much to learn and much that's fresh and new to enjoy.

Throughout this book, I will use the pronoun "her" as I use my new daughter for many examples of bonding. My goal is to keep this personal and easy to read. As I bond with her, I will make notes and include them for your consideration.

I won't bore you with facts and figures from numerous studies about bonding between fathers and their newborns. Trust me; there are mounds of information on this subject, with more coming out each day. I will mention some of the basic research results as they pertain to you and your child, but only in making a point or to emphasize importance.

Each newborn is an opportunity to build a bond that will last a lifetime. Clinical research is fine and serves its purpose, but this new life that is on the way brings an opportunity for you as a father to build a lifelong bond with this child. Dive in and learn the easy and exciting ways to bond with your baby.

Let's go!

Chapter 1: My Bonding Experiences

Each baby has a unique personality. No two are alike. I've chosen to present this fact to you by introducing you to my family. While my situation may not be just like yours, I'm sure I have issues and challenges similar to most fathers out there.

What follows is who I am, how I was raised and how my own family dynamic is structured. I hope this information will help you to be comfortable with who I am and what I'm writing.

I don't have the benefit of any formal education on the subject of bonding with newborn babies. I graduated from the school of hard knocks with a major in fatherhood experience.

I encourage you to note that, over the years, I missed many opportunities to bond with my children, just as my own father missed chances to bond with me. I enjoy a good relationship with my father today and he's a wonderful grandfather to my children. We simply didn't start out on the right foot and this cost us years of strained relations. One of my goals is to help you avoid the same (or worse) scenario with your children.

As I was growing up, my father had little involvement in my daily life. Since I was his only son, this emotional distance wore on me. By the time I was eight years old, I was an angry child. I vowed never to become anything like my dad: a vow I maintained into adulthood. My father worked hard and provided for the family, but I recall only one instance when he and I had some one-on-one time.

Hey! Do you have a license to shoot that thing?

I was in the 7th grade and had just made the junior high basketball team. My father and I were at the police lodge for a picnic (he was a city policeman). The lodge had a nice full-court basketball setup. We spent a couple hours shooting hoops. He could dribble well and had an excellent set shot. (When he was young, jump shots were not as in vogue as they are today.) I was amazed to find out my dad actually knew what to do with a basketball. At thirteen I didn't even know my father could play a sport, that's how distant we were from one another.

That was it: the one real father-son moment I remember. I'm sure he tried to bond with me at other times, but they don't stand out for me. His efforts were limited and very sporadic.

Today, many years later, my father and I have a closer relationship, but it's nowhere near what it could or should be. Fortunately, my household also included my mom and my three sisters, with whom I did have close relationships. That helped me to understand and relate well with women.

When I was thirty-two years old, I married my wife, Bobbie. I thought I was mature enough and ready for the challenges of fatherhood, but there remained a distinct void in the father-role-model area. Bobbie had a nine-year-old daughter, Theresa, and a five-year-old son, Robert, each from previous marriages.

My experience with Theresa and Robert taught me that bonds are difficult to forge when you begin that late in a child's life. It's still possible to build them, but the work is much more difficult and the acceptance from the children depends on many factors often beyond your control.

I adopted Robert, but Theresa's father was actively involved in his daughter's life, so the need to be an adoptive father was never an issue. I began my fatherhood adventure both as a step father and a father through adoption. Looking back, I can see that bonding with these two children would have been drastically different had I been in their lives from day one. Bonding strategies with older children is the subject of another book altogether.

In 1995, Bobbie gave birth to Ivy, our first child together. It had been nine years since Robert's birth and Ivy struggled with breastfeeding. We switched to formula after about eight weeks of frustration on Bobbie's part. I didn't know it at the time, but this gave me one of my first great opportunities to bond with my baby, since it allowed me to do some of the 2:00 a.m. and evening feedings. I burped my daughter and even learned to change her diaper. I felt a strong emotional attachment to her, which grew the more I interacted with her. Fortunately, the fact that I was involved helped build a good bond that we enjoy today at her ripe old age of twelve. Even so, I missed more opportunities to bond with Ivy than I took advantage of.

A couple of years after Ivy, my son Nicholas was born. Nick was a delightful baby, not prone to crying loud and long like Ivy, and quick with a smile. He had a great attitude for a newborn. He quickly grew big and strong and walked early, at eight months. As with Ivy, I missed significant opportunities to bond more closely with Nick due to work, stress and a bleak financial picture. These intrusions, combined with my struggles to bond with my older children, put a strain on the entire household.

We moved to Florida in 1998. About ten months later, Alexandra was born. By this time we owned our own business and our time commitment to it was huge. I used this burden as an excuse for missing chances to bond with Allie and interact with my other children.

Now, six years later, Veronica, (daughter number four) has arrived, and I have taken stock of everything I learned about parenting over the years. I recognize there are many areas in which I could be a better father, so I have decided to focus on maximizing my strengths and shoring up my weaknesses. It is my goal to form strong bonds with my children that will last a lifetime.

I wrote this book about bonding with a newborn from a new father's perspective. As I looked for ideas on bonding between newborns and fathers, I found the information to be limited. The majority of advice available to men about bonding is written either from a clinical perspective or with mothers in mind. I'd be the last person to tell you to discount the many good things you can learn from the mother of your child. Mothers tend to form a natural bond early because they are so intimately involved as caregivers. But I wanted dad-to-dad tips on simple things I could do to get closer to this special little package that stepped into our lives in late 2005.

Coincidentally, Veronica had arrived in the midst of a career change that took me into the world of writing. I took the advice of a friend and decided to apply my writing skills toward my parenting experience – and this book was born. I find that as I write this book, my bond with Veronica, my sixth child, develops rapidly.

For this book, I culled all the bonding information I could find, searched for everything I could learn from others and included ideas I've used over my fifteen years of fatherhood. In my experiences of bonding with my children, if I haven't seen it, heard it, felt it or smelled it I would be quite surprised. If, by writing this book, I can help even one father build a closer bond with his child, then my mission will be a success.

No matter how much wisdom this book contains, attempting to bond from a recliner while thumbing through these pages simply won't work. Hands-on training is the single most important way to learn how to bond with your newborn. This book is designed to give you directions you can use to get involved in bonding with your infant immediately. Trust in your efforts even if you don't see results right away. Remember, this is a long-term commitment. Don't wait as long as I did to be the best father you can be for your child. Read this book, apply the simple tips provided within and *revel* in the growth of your precious child.

Chapter 2: Getting Started

The best way to enter into fatherhood is to plan. Sit down and discuss with your mate when and how many children you would like to have. Make sure your everyday life patterns are as close to supporting a good family dynamic as they can possibly be. My wife and I did just that with our first child, Ivy. The following three are another story completely.

Nicholas was only half planned. We knew we wanted another child, we just weren't sure when. He came somewhat of a surprise in December 1996. Alexandra was a complete surprise in 1999 and Veronica was our last child for the third time.

I'm going to suggest in this chapter that you step in right from the beginning and learn all you can from doctors, nurses, mothers, books and your baby. Get involved in the doctor visits, Lamaze and other pre-birth learning experiences. Take note of the importance of bonding with Mom first. Above all, do not be shy once your baby is born. I'm going to give you specific examples of what to do and expect when your baby is born and what not to do.

Where to start

The best place to start is at the beginning. For the purposes of this book, the beginning is the time when you start planning the birth of your child.

"Do people actually do this?" you may ask. My answer is, "Absolutely." Here's a great example. Bobbie already had a nine-year-old daughter and five-year-old son when I married her. After a couple years, we discussed having another child and decided to move forward. We began to plan for our first child, Ivy. We arranged our lives so we would be prepared for the new arrival. A medication I was taking at the time restricted my sperm count, so for two years we failed to produce a child. Finally, we calculated the day that we had the best chance of success for fertilization and we abstained completely from intercourse until that perfect moment arrived. It actually worked; Bobbie became pregnant! So after two years of planning we were now preparing for the birth of our child. Sometimes circumstances make you very happy you had a plan.

Bonding with Mom

Bonding with Mom is the beginning of bonding with your child. I attended Lamaze classes with Bobbie and learned many things about what a woman's body endures during pregnancy. It is truly eye-opening for a new father, and I recommend participating in a Lamaze class with your wife. I went with Bobbie to her OB checkups. I asked questions, listened to our baby's heartbeat and marveled at her sonogram images. I learned about the different trimesters and how the baby progresses through each, and I talked with my wife about the changes going on inside her. On the day of my daughter's birth, I was a reasonably informed father-to-be about the mechanics of childbirth.

But was I ready for Little Miss Ivy when she was born? Absolutely not! My job in retail management called for long hours dealing with the public (especially the complaining public), on a daily basis. When I returned home, stressed and wearied, this little baby I had planned out with my wife destroyed every notion I had about being a father. She screamed at all hours of the day and night. My wife tried to breastfeed her, without success, so we switched to formula. She wanted to be fed every two hours. She needed diapers changed, it seemed, about as often. She did not smile even once during the first month of her life. I eventually learned this is normal, not a youthful comment on a newborn's surroundings. I stressed. My wife stressed. The two older children stressed. So, before you follow in my footsteps, let's back up and find out how some of that stress could have been completely avoided.

The delivery room

The day Ivy arrived, my wife and I had to walk through the hospital corridors for about five hours to encourage the progress of labor. When walking was no longer possible, I was in the delivery room coaching her, using Lamaze techniques. A couple of hours later, I was in tears as I saw my daughter for the first time. I cut the umbilical cord and, as they say, my life was forever changed.

When Ivy was born I was shocked and a little concerned that she was purple, but to me it was a pretty shade of purple, at least. She came out purple because she had been enclosed in a liquid environment for over nine months. Her skin had never been exposed to light and air. Thus she was purple, but within minutes her color began to normalize.

I should have held my new daughter every chance I got. But she was so small in my hands, I was fearful I would hurt her. **One of a new baby's primary means of bonding is through touch,** and my reluctance to hold Ivy initially was a lost opportunity to bond with her. I let the "experienced" mom do the bulk of the caregiving. It was several days after Ivy's homecoming before I actually began to hold her with confidence.

Timing is very important. Infants don't stay infants for long. You have a few brief months to experience this stage of your child's life. I've watched three of my children grow so quickly it's made my head spin. Now that I'm blessed with a fourth baby, I'm truly learning how precious this fleeting time is. Too often we hear people say, "Enjoy your baby while you can." Guilty of not doing this to the fullest in the past, I'm using the opportunity afforded me by Veronica to bond as deeply as I can with this newest addition to our family.

Already three weeks into her life, Veronica will fall asleep in my arms whenever she gets fussy. She seems to understand that when I pick her up, I'm not necessarily going to feed her as a reaction to her crying, but that I will take her outside on walks or let her nestle on my right shoulder and she'll be safe. We've developed a connection through consistent and loving touch.

Mom and Dad begin together

A new mother and father are equally inept at bonding with their first child. I know this might be contrary to everything you've heard, but studies have shown this to be true. The woman who carries your child for nine months really has no leg up on you the day your child is born. In fact, I discovered my wife had forgotten many of the bonding techniques she had learned from her experiences with the older children. She also was unaware of many new techniques that we discovered together.

Touch – one of the ties that bind

Strong bonds are first formed through touch, by holding and feeding the child. Mothers feed the baby more often than dads, comfort the baby and change her diapers. The baby becomes more familiar with her through touch. Since babies cannot focus their eyes beyond a few inches in the first weeks of life, they become accustomed to Mom's touch. They can't even see colors during the first couple of months. Touch becomes a strong component of the bonding process. To minimize the gap in "touch" bonding, dads need to make sure they spend significant amounts of time holding, touching, feeding, changing and even sleeping with their babies on their chests.

In this chapter, I've emphasized that having a plan is a very good idea. A plan can smooth out some of the bumps that are going to pop up.

Getting involved from day one is crucial. The doctor visits and Lamaze classes may not always be convenient, but the effort establishes your mindset to bond at the highest level possible with your baby.

Bonding with Mom is one of the key steps to learning to bond with your baby. What affects Mom while she's pregnant also affects the baby. Take the time and be involved with everything going on inside your mate.

Touch. You will read over and over how important this aspect of bonding is to your baby. Don't be timid. Your baby is amazingly made. Pick her up. Carry her at every opportunity. Do this from the moment she is born.

Chapter 3: Bond During Feedings

In this chapter I make comparisons to moms and I encourage dads to accentuate the ways in which they're different from moms. This is not a divisive way of looking at bonding. It's also not intended to portray a competition between parents. I will say this more than once in this book: your baby already has a mother, give her a father. The two of you, working as a team, will be much stronger parents for the effort. You as a father have different physical qualities from Mom. Your baby needs to experience these qualities so that she'll be able to understand her world and how it works at an early age.

I'll give you a lot of ways to include yourself even when Mom is breastfeeding. Feel free to develop your own. The important issue in this chapter is that you remain involved with and connected to your baby during feeding.

Food – a basic need

One of your baby's most basic needs is nourishment. Babies feed every two to three hours during their first few months of life and you need to be there as often as you can. Eating is one of the most important bonds we share together as humans. When you invite people over for dinner, you do so because you have a special bond with them, or a desire to build one. This is true even more so with your infant. A baby's need for food is one of the most driving forces in her little life.

I recommend that the mother breastfeed your baby. Breastfeeding means your baby will have less gas (less pain and crying), be healthier (stronger immune system) and will be more alert in exploring her environment. There are many opportunities for Dad to bond during breast feeding.

Deliver your baby to her food source

One way is for you to pick up your child when she's ready to eat and carry her to Mom. This act associates you with the feeding process. Another would be to interact with the baby while she's feeding. An infant likes to fall asleep while nursing; it's often hard for her *not* to fall asleep because she's being held by a warm, loving mother. This can be very frustrating for Mom, however, as the child hasn't really had enough to eat. When Mom tries to lay your baby down to sleep, most often the little one will wake up crying because she's still hungry, hence the frustration. So if you interact with your baby and keep her engaged, you're connected to the feeding process and you help Mom out as well.

> *Touch and speech are direct bonding builders. Any time you engage your baby on these two levels is a major benefit for her. Babies are learning about their environment all the time. Become part of her environment and you'll bond nicely with her. By involving yourself in the breastfeeding activity, you're stepping into your baby's environment and making yourself known to her.*

Interactive ways to bond while feeding

Several years ago with my second child (Nicholas), I began dribbling his head whenever I noticed him falling asleep at Mom's breast. By dribbling, I mean I placed my hand on the back of his head and pushed it toward my wife's chest lightly, in a dribbling motion, like in basketball. I always made sure I spoke at the same time, usually saying something ridiculous like, "Dribble, dribble, dribble." My son would wake up and, since he still had a mouthful, he would resume eating, which Mom appreciated. The reason I always said something was so he would know who was messing with his head. These connections to the feeding process are important.

Burping as bonding

Another opportunity to bond is to take over burping duties from Mom. Burping reduces the amount of pent-up gasses that will make your baby cry. I have seen my children's faces twisted in pain due to gas trapped in their stomachs. Babies should be burped every five minutes or so during feedings. Mom may get into an emotional rut and just be interested in finishing the feeding. That's where you come in. When I burp my baby, I cradle her in my right arm so her head is over my right shoulder. I pat her back with my left hand, lightly, but with enough force to help settle out the gas bubbles that may be trapped in her stomach. This is almost an art and people often brag about how well they burp babies.

Burping your baby is another instance in which I'd have some practice under my belt before volunteering for a solo performance. But once you put in the practice, I highly recommend that you actually use your new skills. One-on-one time with your baby may not come about often, so take advantage of any opportunity to spend time alone with her. Mom will most definitely appreciate the time off. If you assume some of the duties of caring for your baby on a regular basis, Mom may not feel the need to seek out those "traffic jams" on the way home.

Bottle feeding

Here's another tip for those fathers whose children are breastfed: have Mom pump out some milk and then *you* can feed your baby with a bottle. Remember, feeding time is a huge bonding time for a baby. All the senses come into play: touch, eye contact, speech, taste, and smell. You want to be as involved as possible.

Bottle nipples are merely substitutes for the real thing. Finding one your baby prefers may be challenging. Be patient and willing to try nipples of varying shapes and sizes until your baby is satisfied and takes the bottle from you. When you're there supplying the food she needs, you've climbed way up on the bonding ladder.

If your baby is taking formula you need to familiarize yourself with how to mix up and heat her formula. Babies will not take it cold. If your child is breastfed like mine, you need to know how to go about thawing and heating the milk Mom expressed for you and stored in the refrigerator or freezer.

This pays off big time when you tell Mom you'll watch the baby while she escapes for a few hours. She may even decide to enjoy herself an hour or two longer than you were expecting. If you've done your homework and know how to prepare your baby's food, you'll have prevented loads of stress. (Ok, she really may have been tied up in traffic!) Do a few practice runs on feeding your baby before you volunteer for this chivalrous act.

Be aware that babies prefer certain positions while they feed. Learn how your baby likes to be held for her meal. She may prefer your left arm or she might like to be propped up with you facing her. Whatever position she likes, go with it. Remember to burp your baby often during her meal. After a good

burp, feel free to resume the feeding process if she's still hungry. She'll let you know she's done by simply refusing to eat any more.

Beyond holding and feeding

When you're feeding your little one, go beyond merely holding baby and bottle. Get involved with your baby. I noticed my wife would clean up an eye that had dried sleep on it, play with the baby's hand or interact in other ways. Sometimes she would talk and sing softly to her. No doubt the singing came when Mom wanted the baby to sleep. Other times she would simply get into a staring contest. What do you think? Can you do those things? Of course you can!

When Alexandra was a wee one, we used to get into staring contests. She had (has) the biggest brown eyes I've ever seen. As she got older and entered into the toddler stage, we would play "big eyes." Whoever could present the "biggest" eyes would win and knock the other over. This, of course, was great fun to her and would inspire many fun-filled laugh fests. She still has the prettiest eyes I've ever seen.

Babies love looking at faces and exploring the differences between Mom and Dad. As dads, our faces have texture, such as beards. As your child grows and begins exploring her world through touch, allow her to learn the rich textures of your face, hands and arms. Make faces at her. Try and copy her face when she does something interesting. But remember, early on her sight is limited, so she may not be seeing what you think she's seeing.

Another critical time for you to imprint your presence on your child is between four and six months when a baby may be ready to begin eating solid food. This doesn't mean she'll be totally off breast milk or formula, but it's another important milestone. Can you hazard a guess as to why?

Of course! You can now actively feed your child without Mom's assistance. Your bond with your baby is enhanced even further and you earn more brownie points with Mom. Dads tend to be very creative during mealtimes while moms are much more straightforward with the feeding of their children. Dads have another opportunity to set themselves apart by making this time a grand experience. While the process can get quite messy, feeding time can be loads of fun for both you and your baby.

You know what I'm talking about—the choo-choo-train-spoon of pureed pears and the airplane load of smashed carrots that flies into your baby's open mouth. These fun times give Mom a chance to relax. Take advantage of the entire bonding opportunity here. Remember to burp your baby when she's finished feeding. Help her to sleep by rocking or walking with her in your arms. Mom gets more time to nap and recharge and it provides you more bonding time with your newborn.

Here come super sonic carrots!

Stay involved

Babies may lay around a lot, but don't convince yourself there's nothing for you to do until your baby is walking and talking. You have the same opportunities to bond that Mom does. Seize the initiative, roll up your sleeves and get involved. This is especially true for first-time dads. Take heart guys: as previously mentioned, both parents are in a learning phase when the baby is born. If you involve yourself from the beginning, you don't have to take a backseat in the bonding process. Take turns with Mom in the driver's seat. Mealtime is a great opportunity to show your baby you care deeply for her.

Benefits of involved fathers

There's another compelling reason to make a strong, conscious effort to bond with your child. This comes from the "John Tesh Radio Show – Intelligence for Your Life."

> *And here's something you may not know about dads: Men seem to be primed to care for their kids by the same hormone that influences women. So basically, we've always been wired to dote on our kids. And it'll have a HUGE impact on them:*
>
> - *Children involved with dads have better social skills when they reach nursery school.*
> - *They do better on tests in high school.*
> - *A child who's close to Dad is less likely to have a criminal conviction by the age of 21.*
> - *They're more likely to have a contented love life when they're older.*
> - *And children of involved fathers are more likely to care well for their OWN children.*

I think John Tesh's relaying of this information is very important. I read many studies while writing this book and all came up with the same conclusion: children who were very involved with their fathers were much better off than children whose fathers were absent.

It's also worth mentioning that children absorb and learn more about life in their first years than older children and adults. That's why I encourage you to be involved with your baby at *every* age. Feeding time is important. A baby gets hungry and cries for food. This same baby is learning who is alleviating her discomfort. You need to be involved. I've given you specific examples of some of the ways I've stayed involved in the feeding process. Feel free to come up with your own. The most important thing is that you do it.

Chapter 4: Dressing Your Baby

In this chapter, I'm going to make a pointed effort to get you to understand the importance of learning to change your baby's diaper right away. We all have our reasons for not wanting to be involved in this task, but what's at stake is much more important than our aversion to messy diapers. Trust me, once you become proficient in the diaper area of life, the process will become quick and simple. Yes, even easy. Practice makes perfect. We know this from sports. The same principles apply here. When you get involved and repeatedly change diapers you'll find it can be a great time to have your little one's focused attention.

Learn to dress your baby

Before I dive into what has to be one of a father's least eagerly anticipated parental acts, I recommend you first do something you consider to be very basic: dress your child. Sounds simple enough, but getting a squirming, screaming baby into a onesie can be tough. What's a onesie? Glad you asked, because no one ever told me. A onesie is like a body suit that your wife would wear except on a much smaller scale, of course.

While you're changing her clothes, be aware that most babies don't like to have their heads covered up. This even applies to the short amount of time required to lift her shirt over her head. To ease your baby's anxieties, play peek-a-boo while changing her shirt.

How is this activity a bonding technique? In order to change your baby's clothes, you must come into contact with her. You'll also find that it helps if you talk to your baby while you dress her. Make eye contact. Use every precious moment to let your baby get to know her dad. This interaction helps soften the "chore" aspect of getting your baby dressed and puts you more in the frame of mind of seeing this little wonder grow. By the way, you'll be amazed at how quickly she outgrows her outfits.

Have fun during the clothes changing process, especially after the two-month mark, when your baby is smiling. For example, when you're putting socks on your baby, warm her up with a "This little piggy went to market" game.

The dirty diaper

Ok, that was the easy part. Now let's move on to the more challenging aspect: diapers. Whew, they are a nasty business! No one actually likes to change them. Many times I was fully expecting a nasty diaper and was blessed with only a wet one. But there have been the messy ones. There have also been the ultra-messy ones. Then there were what my wife and I called the "blow-outs." Stay calm, you can handle this.

See no diaper...

Smell no diaper...

Changing diapers is an *excellent* opportunity to bond with your baby. By now you know I am going to mention touch, sight and sound, however, I must draw your attention to the stinky aspect of diaper changing. When your baby's diaper needs changed, how do you think she feels? It's not a pleasant thing to be wearing, and if you don't change it quickly, a rash can form. Then you *really* have an unhappy baby on your hands. Besides, in the early months when your baby is breastfeeding or on formula, her diapers will not be all that smelly. This allows you time to get adjusted to diaper changing without the smell intimidating you.

Babies don't like dirty diapers. This is where Dad comes to the rescue. Do you see

Change no diaper!

where I am going here? Not only do you bond with touch, sight, and your voice, you make your baby comfortable again. Babies have a strong need for, a dependence upon, someone to take care of them. By helping your little one feel better, you're strengthening these precious bonds.

Good reasons to change that diaper

Dads should take care of their children by providing a safe, comfortable atmosphere in which to grow. Studies show that infants who bond with their fathers from birth have a much lower incidence of behavioral problems when they get older. They're also more focused on academic achievement. While changing diapers is only a small part of the bonding process, it's critical that you as a father participate in it, thereby deepening your bond with your baby. Let her know that you'll be involved in all aspects of her life. Changing diapers is a small price to pay for the relational bonds you create. As a result, you'll see many positive traits blossom as your baby grows older.

Changing diapers doesn't hurt your relationship with Mom either! Once you change one, you'll change many more. I say this not to scare you, but to encourage you. Again, like dressing your child, remove the "chore" aspect from your thinking. Replace it with the knowledge that not only are you taking care of your precious baby, you're creating a bond that will last a lifetime.

The basics of diaper changing

Here are a few things to know about changing diapers. First, your baby is likely to get upset. Wouldn't you? Often from the moment you lay her down for a changing she's crying. Try and empathize with her. Moms generally do a great job of this, but men seem to struggle a bit here. Understand that once you clean up the mess and put everything back together, the crying will most likely stop.

Second, have wipes and a clean diaper within reach. With my first child, I jumped right in only to discover I had no wipes nearby. I made the situation even worse by trying to hold my daughter's rear end up (lifting her by the ankles with one hand till she was basically standing on her head) as I stretched for the wipes. Of course this caused more crying and squirming, making the job all the more challenging.

Modern-day diapers use a Velcro-like tab to hold them in place. Most have a cartoon picture of some sort on them. Just remember, pictures go up front.

Finally, remember to smile and speak gently to your baby. If you have your wipes and diapers set up and organized, you can focus on soothing your child rather than rushing and panicking. This is one reason why I recommend dressing your child a few times before tackling a dirty diaper. You want to work quickly and efficiently, but you don't want to rush or display an air of panic. Children of *all* ages pick up on these emotions and that perception only serves to complicate the situation.

While you change her diaper, talk soothingly and engage her eyes. Make a connection with your baby while you clean her up. Since you've previously dressed your baby, removing garments will not be a new experience for you. You know what goes where, so dressing her will be easily accomplished. You're rescuing your child from a situation she can't resolve herself, so use this opportunity to connect.

The cleanup

Boys are much simpler to clean than girls. It's important to clean every bit of the mess up, as the resulting rashes and infections from extended contact with feces are simply not good for your baby. Boys clean up with a few good wipes, but girls call for a more detailed effort. This is a sensitive area for your daughter, so be thorough but gentle. Be certain there are no feces left behind. Sprinkle some baby powder on the previously affected area after he or she is cleaned up. This helps prevent chafing and diaper rash. Put a clean diaper on your baby, dress her and then pick her up. If your baby is in her first few months of life, she'll likely still be crying when you're done. Hold her in her favorite position (my daughter Veronica loves my right shoulder) and go to the place in the house that your child finds most soothing. Comfort her by talking softly and holding her lovingly.

A quick aside here: Be aware that the remains of her umbilical cord will be attached to your baby for approximately two weeks. It will be black and continue to shrivel until it falls off. This is normal. When changing a diaper, care must be taken to fold the front of the diaper down, exposing the cord to air.

Bonding during a diaper change

At the conclusion of a diaper change, you'll have used the basic techniques all babies need for bonding: touch, voice, eye contact. You've rescued your child from a most uncomfortable situation and made her feel better physically. Most important, you took the time to soothe her emotional distress.

Why have I spent so much time on the diaper issue? Let's face it, guys: if left to our own devices, we would delegate the diaper changes because they're unpleasant. I hope I've offered a different perspective. Diaper changes are a treasure trove of bonding opportunities. When you change your baby's diaper, you have the opportunity for emotional connections. She associates you with someone who will take care of her. You also make a physical connection with her and, most importantly, you're stepping in and taking charge.

Our children need to see more interaction from their fathers. Look at fathers on television these days. Most of them are dolts who don't step in and bond properly with their child. They can't even think to feed their baby, much less change a diaper. They're also portrayed as incapable. If you don't wish to be associated with these father-figure caricatures down the line, get involved now. Where bonding is concerned, consistent involvement pays the largest dividends.

So, are you convinced? Your baby is pleased and happy that you've rescued her, the same thing can be said of Mom and you're proving that you're a father who's involved in all aspects of childrearing. I don't mention this so you can stand up and pat yourself on the back, but so that you can see yourself as a dad who takes charge and handles an unpleasant situation competently and lovingly. We're not buffoons. We're fathers who love our children.

Chapter 5: Spending Time with Your Baby

Now we're going to explore some of the ways a dad gives his time to his baby. This chapter does not by any means cover all the myriad ways possible to spend precious time with her, but it does give some concrete ideas. You'll have your own ideas for ways to interact with your son or daughter. The most critical thing is to act on the ideas.

When you make the effort, even if things don't work out the way you expected, both you and your baby are learning how to grow closer. As a writer, I know an idea is nothing more than a dream, a nonexistent fantasy, unless you put action to it. Your baby needs your time more than you could ever imagine. Look at the various ways I present here to invest time in your baby, and come up with some of your own.

A healthy dose of time

In the United States, we seem overly concerned about spoiling our children. In many cultures, parents rarely put their babies down, carrying them all day in a sling or a front pack and sleeping with them at night. Your baby loves and craves your touch, your voice and your attention. She feels your warmth and is secure as you make contact with her. I think we're so concerned about spoiling our children that, ironically, we err on the side of not giving them enough attention. Stroke your child and give her big, warm hugs. Spend as much time with her as you can fit into your day. She craves this attention and you should give it to her in healthy doses.

I primarily mention touch, voice and eye contact as bonding opportunities. Yet they all have something very basic and integral in common: they take time. You will not bond with your child, at *any* age, if you don't spend time with her. Remember, moms typically spend many hours with their children; dads typically don't. The more *time* you lovingly give to your child, the stronger your *bond* will be. These two are inseparable. Your time spent with your baby translates directly into a stronger bond with her.

Be available to your baby

I know this tip is self-evident and a time-honored classic, but it's nonetheless critically important. Cuddle her. Rock her in your arms while singing or humming. Talk to your baby. Do not cut this time short; the television and newspaper will always be available. Take twenty minutes, a half hour or even longer and practice putting your baby to sleep. This transmits love and tenderness to your child at a level that's universal. Guys will be guys, but don't rob your baby of tenderness from her father.

Another interesting tip is to use warmth. If you're attempting to calm her down and nothing else is working, try tossing a receiving blanket in the dryer until it's quite warm, but not hot. Take it out and wrap her up. The change in temperature to something warmer may just be the ticket to calming her down.

> *Cuddling and rocking your baby in your arms is understood by people everywhere as an expression of love, no matter the continent or culture. Something this universal has to be effective.*

Swaddling your baby is an effective tool we've used with Veronica. Swaddling changes her warmth factor. To swaddle your baby, wrap her up in a soft receiving blanket, arms at her sides. This makes her look very tubular. Babies enjoy the security of feeling contained in something warm. Considering where they just came from, that is most understandable.

When a bad day goes worse

The stress of the day has Mom ready to erupt, plus the baby is angry and upset, drowning out the television or radio with her screams. All you want to do is relax after a hard day's work by reading the paper, watching the news, or enjoying your favorite TV show. Remember, as a father you must make sacrifices for the sake of your baby. This is a responsibility that should not be ignored. Unfortunately men today seem inclined to shirk their responsibilities and just let Mom handle everything. Everyone loses in this scenario, and it simply doesn't have to be this way. Take time to be an involved father by stepping in and relieving Mom for awhile. Everyone wins when you do this.

Babies' early responses

During the first two months of her life, your baby will likely give you little feedback other than crying and quiet. This makes it important for you to persevere and stay the course even when its effectiveness is not obvious. Keep using the bonding opportunities listed in this book with the knowledge that somewhere inside her pretty little head, your daughter is bonding with you. One day you both will have something to show for your efforts.

Direct feedback from your child will come all too soon. Take advantage of these early months, when she's most impressionable, to impact your baby by spending time getting to know her. Hang out with her even when it appears nothing you do affects her very much. There are instances right now when I question whether Veronica can even hear. I talk to her but I can't get or hold her attention or keep eye contact with her. Experience, though, tells me she's assimilating my voice and soon she'll respond to it in ways I would expect. I've learned patience. I truly hope this knowledge will help you when you question whether anything you do is of significance to your baby. Trust me on this one. See it through and one day you'll be thankful for your efforts. So, too, will your baby.

The hectic life

The world we live in is fast-paced and results-oriented. Too often, unless we see immediate fruit from our labor, we move on to something else. With children you're making a lifetime investment and may not see the benefits of that investment for years. I believe this is one reason fathers aren't more involved with their babies at the earliest stages of their lives. While this may seem like an obvious reason, it's not a good one.

Fathers today need to reclaim their role in their babies' lives. Too many studies show that the lack of a strong father figure has detrimental effects on children. This also increases the burden on Mom. In addition, our youth get more and more dissatisfied with family life each day. You read about it in magazines, newspapers and see it on the evening news, talk shows and documentaries. You see evidence of it on blogs and websites produced by young people themselves. Fatherhood is a responsibility just like motherhood. It should not be entered into lightly, even if it is accidental. Too often, the mother bears all the responsibility in raising children. This burden forces many mothers to pick their areas of concentration. Many parental duties, such as the discipline children need to grow up stable and secure, are compromised.

Invest your time wisely

As a father, you need to invest time to provide a solid, reliable source of love, information, support and trust for your children. The older you get as a parent, the more you realize this baby will be taking over from your generation. This includes every single function of society. Work, leisure, sports and anything else you can think of that you do right now will be their domain in the future. You can choose to have an impact on

Our future is in their hands!

this future, or you can allow your baby's future to unfold at random, driven by the whims of society.

More and more I see how the time I spend teaching, encouraging and bonding with my children will become so very critical in just a few years. You often hear people say, "Oh my, they grow so fast!" I have experienced this. You simply can't believe how quickly the years pass. One day, before you're ready, you'll be escorting your daughter down the aisle. This is the same daughter that yesterday, it seems, was grinding snack crackers into your carpet as she learned to crawl.

Day care

When Ivy was born, we had to put her into day care while my wife and I went off to work. A friend of ours watched a number of children in her home. We would drop her off each day and pick her up on our way home from work. Mornings were always difficult as she would get the saddest look on her face and cry. Evenings with my daughter were some of the greatest experiences I have had as a father. She would cry out, "Daddy!" (once she learned how to speak) and I would know love on a level that is unconditional.

When it's time for your child to begin day care, you, her father, should be involved in dropping her off and picking her up as often as possible. This develops trust between you and your baby. By consistently being involved, she'll come to trust that you'll return for her. She'll learn to have faith in you.

Work is not an excuse

Work takes up so much of our time as adults; just imagine the added time commitment of a baby. Until you've become a father, you can't fathom how much of a distraction your little one will be. The boss calls and asks you to work the weekend, or you have to work overtime to pay the bills or complete a project. You come home exhausted, but you look at Mom and you realize she needs a break.

This is where the rubber meets the road. You need to willingly give some of your time to your precious baby. How do you do it? Your baby doesn't want to hear your horror stories of being overworked, any more than your boss wants to hear that you want more time to play with your child.

Even if you do tell your baby about your day, her primary desire is still your time. Make it a habit to interact with your baby no matter the circumstances. Here is where you'll have to be strong-willed in your commitment to view this as an enjoyable, bond-building act. You shouldn't resent the time you give up. So go ahead and tell her about your day. Explain how exhausted you are and how much you'd just love a hot shower and a nap. The sound of your voice and the warmth of your touch are things your baby needs from you. Work hard to maintain a "dad" perspective, one that's loving and giving to your child. She won't understand a word you say, but you'll feel much better. This also teaches your baby language and speech patterns, which I'll cover later.

When it comes to committing time to your baby, work can be a convenient cop-out. Don't allow it to muscle in on your time with your baby. I know the bills have to be paid, and there are pressures and aggravations related to your job. Don't allow them to rob you and your baby of the once-in-a-lifetime gift of a strong, unbreakable bond.

So, after the impossible twelve-hour shift you just worked, you may need to stoke yourself up during the drive home, thinking of different ways to interact with your baby. I've often found that my baby is the ultimate cure for a bad day. When you take the time to interact with your baby in a positive way, your day will improve and she'll love you for the effort.

Mimicking is fun and educational

At two months old, Veronica loves to mimic my exaggerated facial expressions. I rapidly flick my tongue in and out, making a funny noise, and she begins to stick her tongue out as well. While she's not very quick, she still gives it a shot. We smile at each other a lot while we play this little game.

I also play another little communication game with her. I make sure we have solid eye contact, then I open my mouth, pause, and breathe out onto her face the word "hi." After repeating this several times, she'll often mimic my mouth position and attempt to say "hi" herself.

Just after Veronica turned eight weeks old, while my mother was visiting, she actually did say "hi." It would have been hard to convince my wife of this had my mother not been there. My wife remains a little skeptical, but she has granted that Veronica may have actually mimicked the word "hi." I tried daily to get her to repeat her success but, four days later, I was still looking for a second greeting from my lovely little baby.

Use technology for future reminiscing

As your baby gets older, she'll be able to visually focus on more objects in her life. Here's a great bonding opportunity for dads: videos and pictures. When old enough, a picture of her, Mom and you will elicit a finger pointing and the act of recognition.

Get a good picture or video of your daughter as she cocks her head to one side and quizzically contemplates her own visage. You'll remember this for the rest of your life and can share the event with her later. Her self-awareness is a special thing to observe in your baby. It makes you want to reach out and hug her. So do it!

Play games

Everyone recalls the games we played as little tykes. Peek-a-boo, the flying airplane, light tickling and a choo-choo train are all-time baby favorites. Make sure you take the time to play these games with your baby before she outgrows them. It's incredibly special to hear your baby giggle. Experience it once and you'll be hooked for life.

> *Make up games that make your baby laugh and smile and giggle. Laugh and smile and giggle along with her and you forge the bond even deeper.*

One of life's sad truths is that we lose this uninhibited ability to giggle and laugh. I don't know where it goes, or when, but go it does and all too soon. I'm thrilled to have the opportunity to experience Veronica's belly laughs and giggles. One of my other daughters, Allie, was quite the giggler in her day. Now she's seven and I just realized she no longer giggles and laughs as freely. She still laughs, and very pleasantly I might add, but it's not with the same unabashed glee that a baby and toddler have. Enjoy this time, please. It will disappear quickly.

Capture the fun

My wife and I chose to have little children running around all our adult lives. However, if you're not planning to have more than one toddler underfoot over twenty-five years of your life, take this precious little time available to you and treasure it.

If you can, get video and audio of your baby laughing. What a lifelong present that would be! Since they don't laugh all the time, that means you must be involved. Make it happen. Play games.

Loosen up and be willing to be a child again yourself. I'm not talking hours on end here, but invest more than five minutes of your time each day. Even better, give your baby a half hour of undivided attention here, an hour there, which gives Mom thirty minutes of relief here and an hour there to relax.

Avoid the waiting game

Don't put off bonding with your baby until she can talk. It's extremely difficult to play catch-up later on and there's no guarantee you'll even have the chance, depending on what's happening between your child and her environment. Sure, you can wait until she's three or four years old, but you're still going to have to build the same bonds I'm talking about here. The difference is that if you wait, she'll have learned that you're not an involved father and you're going to have to overcome that issue while trying to forge these bonds. I'm not saying it can't be done, but obviously you're going to have to work harder then. I learned this lesson when I married my wife whose two children were five and nine years old at the time.

Don't get caught in the trap of thinking once your baby is walking and talking it will be easier to connect with her. Children get progressively more complicated as they grow. Each age has its own set of needs and adjustments. You may find the complexities of child-rearing working against you at times. It's much easier to form a bond with her by investing time up-front when she's a baby. This allows you to develop the connections that will help her through the various challenges of growing up.

What challenges am I talking about? One issue is sharing with siblings and friends. Then there are the complexities of forming friendships and relationships with neighbors who may not make good friends. If you're not in touch with your child from the cradle on, your influence won't carry as much weight when these difficult moments arrive. Take the initiative and get involved! This is going to be beneficial to you both in the form of a strong bond as life moves forward.

Walking is great fun

Take your baby for a walk. There are many opportunities for you to take a walk with your infant, like after dinner or when you get home from work. Walking has been proven to be one of the most beneficial exercises we can do as humans. It reduces stress, helps you lose weight and also helps to clear your mind.

An even better idea is to see if Mom would like to go on a walk with you and the baby. Remember Mom? Eighty percent of the time she spends dealing with your baby is related to crying. This can make her a frazzled caregiver. She could use a break. This is where your attention to what's going on can pay huge dividends for all involved—you, Mom and baby. Take your child on a stroll to avoid a mom meltdown. Make sure you carry the baby as Mom has probably had enough at this point.

Walking outside with your baby after a meal works off some of that good food and helps you bond with your baby. What else is in this stroll for your little

Going for a family walk is not only a great way to bond with your baby and give Mom a break, it's also a great opportunity for a family talk that can alleviate a lot of stress for Mom. Encourage her to tell you about her day. If she has frustrations and concerns, let her know that you understand and that you appreciate the excellent job she's doing with the baby. Ask her what you can do to help. Create a family dynamic of communication that will benefit Mom, Dad and the baby.

one other than the same basic bonding things you do inside? Babies are little sponges. They absorb new information and ideas every minute of the day. The big outdoors is something we adults take for granted. To your baby, everything is brand new. Outside smells are different from inside smells. The sun is a new concept, as is warmth, light, shade, etc. Breezes kick up and blow across your baby's face. Birds chirping, automobiles driving by, the distant hammering of carpenters and leaves rustling in the trees make for an information smorgasbord for your baby. She contemplates and stores all these perceptions and sensations somewhere in her brain for later use.

She'll associate these experiences with you, her dad. A walk can be a special thing no matter how old she gets. I often walked with my teenage son to help him reduce his agitation over various issues. We had some of our most productive talks while strolling the streets.

Why not begin father and child walks, or family walks, early and bond with your baby in a special way? You're not just holding her, talking to her and playing staring games with her, you're showing her the world.

The importance of your time

Here's a bonding tip I jotted down when I first started putting this book together. It's so ridiculously obvious I hesitated at first to include it. I believe I've stated it in a variety of ways, but it bears emphasis. *Do not wait for an invitation to bond with your child. Jump right in!* The act of spending time with your baby is the beginning of your bonding trek.

If you don't jump in, the inclination to put forth the effort to bond with her is not going to come often, if ever. Mom is going to be frazzled and will most likely dump your baby on you when she's had more than she can handle. That will make your interaction with your child more stressful. Or, thinking you're not interested in pitching in, Mom might opt to go to an extended family member or friend for a break. I can't stress enough the fact that if you wish to form a strong, lifelong bond with your baby, you must get involved immediately. To build the bonds that will last a lifetime, you must give up some of your time and energy.

Now you have some good ideas for spending time with your baby. Remember, you must put ideas into action in order to make them effective. There are most likely an infinite number of ways to interact with your baby. All of them require time and effort. Please take the time—make the effort. Next to your love, these are the two most critical aspects of bonding. I would even submit to you that without spending the time and making the effort, you can't convey love, at least not on a level that solidifies strong relational bonds between you and your child.

Chapter 6: Bonding Dad's Way

Dads have a special role to play with their children. We should relish this role and, yes, become a *role model* for our children. In my mind, one of the key roles we should model is that of a man who bonds with his children. We should show, by example, that a father can be loving, decisive and fun. We should convey that bonding with our children is not a chore but a delight. We should give our daughter a role model so she has a good example of what type of man the future father of her children should be. We should pass on to our son the traits that make up a solid, loving father.

In order to do this, we need to be ourselves and allow our children to see a loving father. In this chapter I touch on a number of suggestions for bonding with your baby in ways that will show her what a good father is. There are many others. Explore them and give your baby the gift of a loving father.

Chores and bonding

Do you have chores to do around the house? I certainly do. So I bought a Snugli® which allows me to keep my baby with me while working inside and outside the house. I rake leaves, sweep the sidewalk, take out the garbage and take care of a number of other basic chores while I spend time with my

baby. When doing your chores, just keep one thing in mind—use common sense and don't break out the power tools or anything else that may endanger or frighten your baby. That would defeat the purpose of taking this time to bond with her.

While your baby was in the womb, her mother's heartbeat was quite evident to her. Therefore, a heartbeat is a comforting sound to which a baby is very accustomed. A Snugli® puts her in a position so that her head rests on your chest and she can clearly hear your heartbeat.

Exercise as a bonding opportunity

Another pretty cool bonding idea is to exercise with your baby. Literally. Pick her up and put her down. You can bench press her while lying on your back or sitting in your favorite chair. These are entertaining ways to keep active and to bond with your baby as well. This helps you develop upper-body strength and conditioning. It also gives your baby new sensations through that ever-present bonding technique of touch. Both your biceps and your baby will love it.

Dad is not just another mom

The modern-day stereotype of inept and distant dads who shirk their opportunities for bonding needs to be banished. You should accentuate the differences between mom and dad to give your baby a more accurate picture of her world. Remember, she's observing it for the first time. Every day brings something new into your infant's life. You need to be there to show your baby a well-rounded view of this world.

Earlier, I touched on the fact that men have different skin textures than women. Men have mustaches, beards, five o'clock shadow and the like. Some of us have calloused hands and hairy chests. Babies use their senses to learn more about their world than you could ever imagine.

Encourage this exploration by letting your baby touch and explore these striking differences from Mom.

By contrast, moms are generally softer skinned, softer voiced and gentler in the ways they interact with children. A father doesn't have to follow suit and try to copy Mom. Allow your baby to interact with you in a manner that is comfortable to both of you.

Dad's games

Dads hold their children differently than moms. We also tend to do more knee-bouncing and light roughhousing than moms. These are good activities that involve the basic bonding techniques of touch and speech, which make them great bonding tips. Most men seem to arrive naturally at the decision to bounce and roughhouse with their children on their own. Making a connection with your baby in a way that accentuates the differences between you and Mom will help you to bond even closer with your baby.

If you took the time to "fly" your baby to Mom when you were taking her to feed, you were forming that bond of trust. The more flights made, the deeper the trust. As your baby gets older, the aerial stunts can become more and more complex, further solidifying the trust bond.

Tug- of- war

By the time your baby is learning to roll over and sit up, she'll be ready for a game that's loads of fun. Play tug-of-war with your baby by giving her your finger to grasp. Make sure she has a soft place to land when she lets go. After she lets go, circle your finger around in the air while you playfully hum to her. Then reinsert your finger into her hand and do it again. This is another way of teaching your new baby that her hands are something she controls. It will also help her to develop the coordination to use them. You can also use a toy to play tug-of-war.

Tick-tock

My children love tick-tock. Tick-tock is a little game I made up when Ivy was a around one year old. At a younger age it probably would have scared her. I would grasp her ankles and pick her up slowly until she was upside down. Then I would swing her like a pendulum saying, "Tick-tock, it's Ivy clock," in a rhythm that matched the pendulum swings. This little game is still wildly popular but I must say it's difficult to do, if not impossible, with Ivy now at twelve years old. She still asks me to do it but she's grown too tall. This game came from a natural building of the trust bond as Ivy was growing from a newborn to a toddler. That she still wants to play it shows that the trust remains today.

Look forward to these games. They create special bonds that will be passed down through the generations. I know my grandchildren will be tick-tocked. That is a great and humbling knowledge. By building trust with your baby from the very beginning, your opportunities for similar and probably grander games are unlimited.

Warning—beware!

One experienced word of advice with *any* physical activity. Dads usually don't think of this until it is too late, so let me warn you now: Beware the recently fed child. If you don't want to wear the meal she's just eaten, take it easy for a half hour or so after the meal. Children will spew—as we call it—and while it's not as bad when they're breastfed or on formula, it can still kill a magically playful moment.

Interesting tidbits

Did you know the time your baby spends on her back is very good for her? When you use a baby chair or a bouncer, you're limiting your baby's mobility. Anything that causes your child to be somewhat stationary is basically a babysitter. It's better to lay her on her back and play with her feet or pump her legs in a bicycle motion. This way she exercises her arms, legs and neck. You want to interact as much as possible, so try to limit the use of baby chairs and bouncers.

The bond of laughter

Make your baby laugh! The many proven benefits of laughter include lower blood pressure, lower stress, stronger immune system and release of the body's natural painkillers. Hey, these are just some of the benefits for you! Just think what it will do for your new baby. Veronica began smiling at about the six-week mark. It will be awhile before she laughs, but when she smiles that huge, open-mouthed, baby smile, you know she's feeling just fine.

One of the tricks of being a good, steady father is to see the humorous side of daily life. Share this with your baby to help both of you enjoy your time together. The biggest benefit of your child's smiling or laughing is it gives you an indication of your child's mood. A smile or laugh tells you everything is A-OK.

Laughter plays a fundamental role in bonding, especially with fathers. Babies will learn to laugh just to keep your attention. Initially they're just purely happy and that happiness will melt your heart. When they laugh to get your attention, this is their way of saying they like your company.

Most babies find everyday items hysterical. I was shocked when my first baby, Ivy, would laugh uncontrollably at a floating balloon. This puzzled me until I realized that a floating balloon defied every life experience my little girl had learned thus far. Floating soap bubbles are another of my children's favorite laugh-inducing items.

All of my children loved when I pretended to be asleep, snoring loudly. When they touched me I jerked awake and they exploded with laughter. Another of my infants' favorite games was for me to give them a "raspberry": I moisten my lips, press them to their stomach and blow, making a flatulent sound. (It seems we develop potty humor at a very early age.) It amazes me how many times you can repeat these things and get the same reaction. You can't help but laugh, yourself, after awhile.

Laughter's benefits

I found in all my years as a father that laughter in the house is one of the most therapeutic and disarming experiences you can have. Everyone benefits from laughter and it can help stabilize stressful situations. As I demonstrated above, you don't have to be a comedian to inspire laughter in your baby. Simple things like balloons, bubbles or blowing on her tummy work just fine. You don't have to yuck it up all the time as that would not be a good balance, but you should incorporate laughter in large doses when possible.

I remember, twenty some years ago, playing with my nephew Erik, who was about one year old. I would set him up in his bed and "bop" him gently in the face with a pillow, knocking him onto his back. Erik would laugh as only a one-year-old can. He would raise his arms after a prolonged fit of laughter and shout, "Pillow! Pillow!" I would prop him back up and then "bop" him again and he'd repeat, "Pillow! Pillow!" To this day I have a special bond with Erik. It all began with a game that made him laugh.

My younger sister has a daughter, Amanda, who I bounced on my knee from a very early age. As I bounced her, I would chant, "Doo-doo-doo, doodaloodaloo." No matter when I saw her, the cadence was always, "Doo-doo-doo, doodaloodaloo." As soon as she began to speak she dubbed me Uncle Doodaloo. Guess what my name is fifteen years later. Yep. Uncle Doodaloo. These are special bonds you can make with your child. While you may not want to be called "Uncle Doodaloo" in public (I don't mind), you do want to hear your playful words (or non-words) come back to you.

Fatherhood is going to be what you make of it. You can choose many different avenues and levels of involvement. I present to you that the most satisfying aspect of fatherhood is when you apply yourself totally, willingly and personally. This means stepping out of your comfort zone at times, but it also calls for you to be yourself. Let your baby learn who you are. Don't try to mimic Mom, but give your baby a more rounded and true picture of her world by involving a completely different person—you—on a deep level. This commitment to bonding deeply with your baby is more and more rewarding as life goes on. When that precious little baby grows up and asks your advice on important matters and obviously values your input, everything you did leading up to that moment is justified and magnified as something priceless.

Chapter 7: Signing

Sign language is not just for doctors, nurses, therapists and deaf people. It's a form of communication that can enhance the bond you're forming with your baby. Don't be intimidated. The signs that facilitate communication with your infant are simple and effective.

The signs are simple because there aren't a lot of elaborate hand motions. Sign language brings many practical applications to your household. Your baby will soon be able to communicate specific things like needing milk, food or water. Your baby will soon be able to let you know other things that are affecting her world. The ability to communicate before learning how to speak is a great benefit.

More important, this is an opportunity for you to shine. You'll be spending time with your little one learning the basics of the language, another wonderful way to bond—intellectually.

When to begin

When your baby is around six months old, I recommend teaching her sign language. Signing is not something we did with our previous five children, but now I wish it had been. Veronica loves to sign and even asks us (by signing) to play the DVD about signing. I'm amazed at how quickly she learned basic sign vocabulary.

We use Bright Minds™—Teaching Signs for Baby Minds™. Please allow me to pass along the promotional advertisement from the Bright Minds™ website:

__Teaching Signs for Baby Minds__™ teaches you how to communicate with your baby or toddler before he or she can speak! These fun, easy-to-follow DVDs show you how to use American Sign Language (ASL) to teach your baby how to communicate wants, needs and observations. Teaching your baby sign language is a gift the two of you can share throughout your lives.

Learning signs can also have a profound effect on your child's developing mind. Researchers have found a 12-point difference in the IQ scores of babies who sign and those who do not. This is a huge difference in IQ scores! Preschoolers who learn to sign also test significantly higher on the Peabody Picture Vocabulary Test: a common assessment of verbal ability used to aid school placement.

When we started teaching Veronica sign language, I was reluctant to get involved. I was concerned that I wouldn't be able to learn to sign and I didn't want another time commitment in my life. As the days and weeks progressed, however, I found signing to be a huge bonding opportunity. Veronica absolutely loves to sign. She laughs whenever we communicate through sign language. Her laugh is one of sheer joy. You can plainly see she is excited about being able to communicate.

Benefits of signing

Veronica's first signed word was "milk." She would get hungry, make the sign for milk and laugh. Aside from being incredibly cute, this was an effective lesson in communication for her. She learned she could convey her wants and needs at six months of age. This is huge. Most children can't let you know what they want until they acquire their first limited vocabulary at around a year to a year-and-a-half old. Veronica learned immediately what the signing DVDs offered her and she has actively used that knowledge ever since.

Signing vs. television

Veronica asks for the signing DVDs and shows little or no interest in regular TV. Our other children watch cartoons, but Veronica isn't interested. However, if we put in a signing DVD, Veronica will sit and watch literally for hours.

Veronica's desire to sign has me playing catch-up. I have learned a lot in the past four months. I now recognize most of what she signs and I can sign a little as well. Veronica will take my hand, lead me to my easy chair, let me know she wants to watch the signing DVD and we sit together signing the ones we like the most. Currently she likes to sign tree, helicopter, red, white, lion, elephant, hurray, mom, dad and several other words.

Another benefit is that she has understood since eleven months old when she has a stinky diaper. She will come tell me she needs a diaper change. While this can prevent a nasty "blow out" situation, the greater benefit is that potty training her should now be much easier. Babies are unaware that they can control their bodily functions. By bringing some level of awareness to your baby, you effectively take a major step toward potty training her.

Time to sign

The time Veronica and I spend together learning to sign is precious. She's so attentive and she always wants to show me how to sign her favorite words. It is also nice to be on a walk with her as she points out her observations of objects or animals she's seen on the signing videos. She especially likes birds and dogs. She also likes to point out trees and wind and whether it's hot or cold outside.

I wish I could convince all new fathers to pick up signing DVDs and learn signing with their babies. I've found it much more interesting than I had originally imagined. Veronica loves our silent language and she makes it clear she appreciates anyone who will take the time to sit with her and learn. Look into it. I've been thoroughly pleased with the activity and I know the bond between my daughter and me has been strengthened because of it.

Signing has almost no downside. The only one I can think of is that you must spend a little time and brain energy learning the language. At the same time, though, you're spending time with your baby, helping her develop intellectually and you're learning something new as well.

The ability to communicate with your baby is a tremendous advantage in these early months. You'll be able to avoid unpleasant diapers and hungry baby screams simply through communication. As with any learning activity, your baby is going to accelerate her grasp of the world and how it works by learning to sign. Through increased communication skills, the two of you will forge a bond that you can build upon as she grows. Having already had two teenagers grow up and move out on their own, I see now where this early establishment of communication lines can pay off in the future.

Please do more than consider teaching your baby sign language. Make it happen. We're building bonds that last an entire lifetime. Communication is critical. Go ahead, bond with your baby through sign language too.

Chapter 8: Music and Dance

In the last chapter I went over the importance of communication and the use of sign language as a means to bond in this critical area. In this chapter I want to encourage you to use a couple other communication techniques. As the chapter title suggests, music and dance are tremendous bonding opportunities.

We communicate throughout our lives in many ways. Talking and signing are obvious ways to communicate, but music and dance are art forms that can often reach much deeper levels and therefore can carry more meaning.

Music has been a tried-and-true bonding experience with all six of my children. In many ways, we influence our children without really thinking about it. We play music and sometimes we dance to it and they observe quietly. If we just take it a step further and involve our babies and children in the music and dance we like, we begin to form a common bond of appreciation.

Music

One of my favorite ways to bond is through music. Rhythms are strong sensations for babies. Studies have shown that exposure to music—and specifically classical music—can translate into adults gifted with perfect pitch. I enjoy playing piano. I'm self-taught and most definitely not a virtuoso, but I do recognize the distinct

> *There are many ways in which you can bond with your baby that are simple and enjoyable. Music and dance are two of the easiest.*

advantage possessed by someone who has perfect pitch. This is something I want my children to have.

Alexandra (our fifth child) and I listened to classical music and watched a Baby Einstein® VHS for years. Now she has a most incredible voice and her sense of rhythm is outstanding. I like to think this wonderful talent is tied to the time we spent together listening to music when she was an infant.

Another great way to bond is to sing or hum. Don't worry about perfect pitch or a great singing voice. Just sing. My children don't seem to mind my note-challenged voice and indeed, save for Alexandra, they are often off-key as well. The important thing is, we share a bond of singing together at Christmas, birthdays, in the car and other special family occasions.

Once again, I strongly encourage you to bond through *all* the senses, including auditory. You never know when it will draw you closer to your child. Use all the bonding tools available to you and dare to dream of impacting your child in wondrous ways.

My older children enjoy reminiscing about things we did when they were youngsters. Even my ten- and twelve-year-olds like to talk about special things that make them feel particularly close to their mom and me, things we took for granted. Now that I'm studying and writing this book about bonding, I see fully how the groundwork that builds relationships is special and meaningful. My children ask to sing the songs we used to sing when they were little tykes, and they also sing these same songs to their younger siblings. So sing away!

Dance

Dance also offers many good bonding opportunities with your baby. I purchased formal ballroom dance lessons for my wife and me and we've been totally blessed by the experience. I was desperate for an anniversary gift and I knew my wife liked to two-step while I was a marginal freestyle rock-and-roller. I never expected to enjoy dancing so much, but it's become one of my favorite family activities. During the first ten years of our marriage I wouldn't even step on a dance floor. Now my wife has to drag me away. While taking these lessons, I shadow danced the steps with Alexandra (who was an infant at the time) in order to practice between lessons. I quickly discovered that she seemed to like the waltz and fox-trot.

As I stated earlier, Alexandra has a wonderful sense of rhythm and is musically inclined. Now, in her second year of ballet lessons, she spins gracefully about the house using the dance steps she has learned during her lessons. Is it possible that our shadow dancing not only created a wonderful bond between the two of us, but also had the added benefit of instilling the gift of dance in her?... I like to believe so.

Dance is soothing

Dancing with your child is soothing and comfortable. The music, touch and even eye contact are strong bonding opportunities. All children relate to music and I strongly recommend the joy of song and dance. By the way, I recommend you continue to dance with your daughters as long as you live and your sons for as long as they will tolerate it.

Humans have enjoyed song and dance throughout history. One of the ways we bond with prospective mates is to dance. While dancing on a date doesn't guarantee that you'll find romantic love, dancing with your baby does insure that a lifelong bond will exist between father and child. By taking the time to introduce music to your baby and help her experience the movements associated with dance, you're bonding by means that are time tested.

Your baby will surprise you by how much she enjoys this style of bonding. One day you may be amazed at how proficient she is in the art of music or dance. Even if life doesn't lead her that way, you'll have a special time that the two of you will remember and I am sure both of you will cherish this bond forever.

Chapter 9: Bathing and Massage

You wouldn't think a bath could be so nerve wracking. Your little baby is terrified of everything from the water to your pensive, fear-drenched face. She starts screaming and you mentally melt down. Not a pretty picture.

It doesn't have to be this way. There are a couple great bonding opportunities that bath time and massages offer you. As usual, they involve an investment of time with your baby. Also as usual, you can bring a lot of playful fun to these activities that will engage your baby and make the time spent special to you both. And they will once again help you assert yourself as a father who's involved with his baby. You can incorporate both of these techniques into your daily routine with minimal inconvenience.

Bath time

Bath time provides a challenge most men shy away from. I used to bathe Ivy leaning over the bathtub, keeping a hand on her at all times because I was terrified she'd fall over and bop her head. I was also concerned about her head going under the water or her crying or any number of other challenges that made bathing her difficult.

One day I had a brilliant idea. Why break my back bending over the tub, getting soaked in the process and ending up with an unhappy, screaming infant on my hands? So I decided to change my position on the subject and I highly advise that you do the same. Climb on into the tub with your child! This gives your baby a strong sense of security. She sees, feels and hears Dad getting in with her—strong, nurturing Dad—and immediately she feels safe and secure.

When you're in the tub with your baby, you can pick her up and put her head on your shoulder or rock her in your arms. This is a good time to play, which all dads seem to be adept at and, hey, you both get clean!

Initially, a bath is a new, perplexing and frightening sensation for a baby and, so, can cause the kinds of problems I mentioned above and create a real struggle for you. Anything you can do to ease your child's anxiety is a big help in making this time special. Once you get into a rhythm, she'll look forward to the time you spend together.

Baby massage

Massage is a natural, simple bonding technique that anyone can do and baby massage is very popular these days. I've read many articles touting this as an excellent bonding opportunity. Babies thrive on touch, making this a wonderful way to engage your little one.

> *It is even suggested by some massage therapists that you begin massage techniques while your baby is still in the womb. Let her begin to know your touch early!*

Gently massage her feet, legs and arms. One of the techniques I like is to write invisible words on my baby's tummy with firm but gentle movements using two or three fingers. My wife enjoys putting lotion on Veronica while she notes ticklish spots for future reference. She talks out loud about her observations while she massages our daughter. By doing this, she is incorporating speech and touch through massage. If Mom can do it, so can you.

So, as a father, you bathe your baby periodically and you massage her when you get a free moment here and there. By doing this, you continue to build your relationship with your baby to a level that will surpass many men who don't realize the importance of being so involved with their children.

When you take the time to bathe your baby and make it enjoyable for you both, a strong bond forms. When you care enough to massage your little one, she remembers. In fact, she will look forward to the next time you come along and bond with her. By being involved, you're going to build an expectation and desire that you be an integral part of her life. Is that not what bonding is all about?

Chapter 10: Soothing a Crying Baby

There are many ways in which you can interact with your baby when she cries. The most important thing is to interact with a calm, loving demeanor. This can sometimes be challenging depending upon your circumstances and what's going on around you. You should claim no excuse for handling your crying baby in anger. I stress in this chapter the importance of staying calm and handling your baby's demands in a controlled, positive way. This is no easy task sometimes, but the better you can be at remaining calm, the easier it will be for you to overcome the many challenges of dealing with a crying baby. I hope my advice in this chapter helps ease you into this area of fatherhood.

There are many upsides to your baby crying, and I hope that by pointing out some of them here, I'll inspire you to take on your unhappy baby with bonding in mind. The strides you make when she's this little help set the framework that will define your relationship later. This is one of the *best* times for you to step in and bond.

Crying babies and stress

I once bought a bib for a relative's newborn that stated, "I coo, I goo, I poo, that's all I do." While quite clever, it's by no means accurate. Babies sleep often and cry even more. In the beginning, with my first few children, I allowed the crying to stress me out. It kept me in a constant level of frustration. Why was this child crying *so much*?

As I became agitated, I caused the baby to become more agitated in turn. Sometimes you don't even realize how stressed you are and how much stress you're transmitting to your child. Babies pick up on both the positive and negative signals in our voices.

Babies cry. The good news is the crying will end. You can help by staying calm. Maintain your composure and explore different ways of calming your baby.

Some simple ways to calm your crying baby

Veronica loves to be walked outside. Since this is also a good bonding technique, if she's crying I'll sometimes begin to calm her with a walk and then move to some other bonding technique like letting her fall asleep on my chest. Children whose dads bond with them feel an aura of safety and peace when they're around their fathers. Your baby feels the warmth of your body as well as the rhythm of your heart. Heartbeats are a familiar sound to newborns since they've just spent the last forty weeks listening to their mother's heartbeat. In addition, your child connects with the rhythm of your breathing. Soft speech serves to calm the child and tighten that bond even more.

I like to use a variation of this chest-sleeping technique with Veronica. While watching a ballgame or show on television, I place her head on my right shoulder as I lean back in my easy chair. She will generally sleep for hours this way and my wife is happy to bring me a drink or snack. Also, with this activity you get to employ your manly expertise with your TV's remote. This frees up Mom to do other things or simply to get away for a little while and remember who she is without a baby attached to her.

Crying – the first couple months

Sometimes when Veronica cries, my wife, Bobbie, goes to bed to get some much needed sleep and lets her cry. Parents develop a *sleep debt* in the first couple months of a baby's life. Once the baby gets to where she sleeps through the night, life regains some normalcy and you can get caught up on sleep.

Your baby will sleep longer periods of time in her second month, but you have to wait until she's on solid food for your peaceful night's sleep to return in full. Just know that the day is coming when she really *will* sleep through the night.

Taking the time to bond with your child instead of "toughing it out" during the sleep deprivation period can make the entire experience much less stressful. Whenever she's crying and both Mom and Dad need some sleep, you be the one to step up and take care of her. This proactive approach has its own special set of rewards as your precious child begins to look at Dad as someone who will always be there for her.

Before writing this paragraph, I was in my easy chair with Veronica asleep on my chest, her little head snuggled on my shoulder. This allowed Bobbie to catch three hours of sleep. This rest was very important for Bobbie since she was coughing as though she were coming down with something. Veronica slept peacefully as did her mother. I didn't get all the sleep I wanted, but I did get the rest I needed.

A quick aside: There is always a concern when Mom gets sick that she'll pass it on since she is in constant contact with the child, especially when breastfeeding. Newborns have a much stronger immune system than older children and are typically safe even if Mom is sick. I experienced this fact with my first three children. During those times when my wife caught a cold or got sick, my babies' health continued to be strong. For this reason, I'm more secure when Bobbie is obviously feeling a bit ill. I hope this information will calm any concerns for a new father in a similar situation. Babies may appear small and fragile, but actually are more protected than we might think.

> *Babies' naturally strong immune system protects them from catching common illnesses easily.*

When nothing works

Potentially, one of a crying baby's most dangerous threats is an overstressed parent. Despite your willingness to bond, the crying-baby aspect of fatherhood does present many challenges. All too often you see on the news or read in the paper about shaken-baby syndrome and other acts of frustration. The most important thing to remember when your child is crying is to *remain calm*. Babies don't die from crying. They *can* get loud! Often, they just want to be held, or they just want to eat. If you've fed your baby, changed her diaper, walked her, danced with her and even sung to her and she still wants to cry, stay calm. This happens to *all* parents, even mothers.

It's important to adopt a relaxed approach. You did the same thing when you were a baby. Your parents faced the same situation. This too shall pass, perhaps all too quickly. If you've done all you can, let her wail. Most likely she'll fall asleep eventually.

Know your baby's cries

Of your baby's cries, the "pain" cry is the most important to figure out, but is easily discernable. So when your child wants to cry and you have determined she's not in pain, do not be afraid to let her wail a bit. Sometimes your precious baby will simply cry herself to sleep.

I wish I could say I handled all my children's crying bouts with calm, disciplined savvy. No one told me to tune the crying out from my emotional side and just approach the tears from a more detached or analytical view. Doing so can reduce your stress levels immensely. Have sympathy for your baby; just remember that sometimes it's important for you to keep your focus and perspective.

Dangers of stressing over a crying baby

One drizzly afternoon, while driving down a two-lane road, my then infant child, Ivy, was wailing from the backseat. Mom was beside me in the front seat. Ivy's eight-year-old brother was sitting beside her, hands over his ears. Mom was frazzled (I had not yet learned the benefits of taking some of the load off her) and I was stressing to the max. In an attempt to be a good dad, I leaned over the backseat and tried to placate my little girl. When I turned back around, a car in front of me had stopped to make a turn. I locked up my brakes but slid into the stopped car anyway. This is proof positive that keeping a level head is in your best interest. Fortunately, no one was hurt.

Do you believe frustration can't or won't happen to you? It probably can, but you can also learn to control your frustration over your child's crying.

Observe how your baby cries

Babies develop rhythms in their attempts to get attention. These days I like to mimic Veronica's rhythmic crying. Her cries are like a sergeant's cadence and by mimicking them the emotional sting is taken out of the situation.

One of Veronica's favorite cries for attention is to sound for all the world like a peacock. If you've never heard a peacock this probably makes no sense, but the point is, I manage to deflect my emotional response to her crying by making it into a little game. Sometimes when I mimic Veronica's peacock cry, she'll stop momentarily and look up at me as if to say, "Wow, you feel it too!" Then we proceed to harmonize.

Separate emotional frustration from crying

I can't stress enough the absolute need to separate your emotional frustration from your baby's crying. You'll reap emotional dividends a thousandfold if you can accomplish this. My wife has noted that when I hold Veronica, she stops crying and often falls asleep. Granted I tend to walk her around which seems to occupy her, but I also think by bonding with her the way I have, she has come to expect security and love from me. Mom, especially since she breastfeeds and is the main caregiver all day, is more a product-bearing person. Typically, 80 percent of the time that mom interacts with her newborn is a result of the baby crying. This fact can help dad be very effective quieting his baby in ways different than mom. A different approach can sometimes be just the calming effect needed.

Benefits of bonding during crying spells

Since I interact more evenly in all phases of Veronica's life—crying, quiet sleeping, etc.—when with me, she expects to be held, walked and encouraged to sleep or observe her world. This is a tremendous boon to me as I have the ability to overcome the fussy, "I just want to be held and I'll raise a stink if I'm not" baby and turn her into the beautiful little girl she ought to be.

Babies cry for four reasons

Babies generally cry for one of four reasons:

- ✓ Pain is one of them. If she bumps her head or hurts herself in any way, all you can do is pick her up, hug her and talk soothingly to her. If you've bonded well, and her injuries are not severe, you can quickly turn off those cries.

- ✓ A dirty diaper is another reason. The sooner you change her (babies are notorious for excreting in stages, so make sure she is finished), the sooner she'll return to playful explorations of life with you as her guide.

✓ Hunger is the third reason for crying. If she's bottle-fed, this is a great opportunity for you to step in and bond on many levels. If she's breastfed, stay involved for a while after feeding starts. Let her make the connection that you brought her to her food.

✓ A desire for attention is the last reason. This cry usually doesn't begin until your baby has learned how to manipulate her world. This is one of the early ways of using her vocal cords to get what she wants.

Recognize the different cries

Recognize the difference between the vocal expression for "I'm hungry" and the one for "I'm hurt." Being involved with your baby will help you to distinguish between these two cries. One key factor I realized just the other day with Veronica is that pain is not a rhythmic cry. It's more forceful and erratic, while the "please hold me" cry is more of a rhythm or a crying chant that can be maintained for a long, long time.

Never underestimate your baby's determination to get what she wants. She can cry and demand to be held for what seems like impossible amounts of time. Parents need to win that battle occasionally, but for the purposes of bonding, make that connection with your baby. Pick her up or change her diaper. You'll be glad you did in the long run.

> *Often in a battle of wills with the parents, a baby will win. They have no agendas, no deadlines and no responsibilities.*

Baby's feelings of security

An infant feels secure when her father responds promptly and appropriately to her cries. Be alert and responsive to your baby. Yes, this often calls for you to step out of your comfort zone. I have news for you: when this baby came into your life, your comfort zone was destined to be squeezed anyway.

Bonding with your child when she's an infant requires effort now, but not bonding with her will require even greater effort further down the road. Children without strong fathers tend to act out more and have more behavioral problems. It's like that old commercial: you can pay me now, or pay me later.

The payoff to bonding with your infant from her earliest moments of life is huge. Your involvement will profoundly affect her life by giving her a sense of trust and security in you as her father. Conversely, children without a father's influence struggle in many areas of life. When you step in and respond to your baby's needs, she'll learn she has a strong and stable foundation which she can stand on for life.

Sleep and the crying baby

When you mention to others that you have a new baby in the house, they're bound to bring up the topic of crying. I bet the question most asked a new father after the first week is, "Are you getting any sleep?" Even mothers often ask this question. In the past, those mothers were likely to have been up all hours of the night for feedings with little help from dad. Don't be stuck back in the stone age of fatherhood. Yes, you'll suffer some sleep deprivation during the first months of your baby's life, but if you stick with it, you'll soon see the good stuff.

In the past couple of months, Veronica woke me up a handful of times with her demand for attention. Writing this book helped me deal better with being woke up in the middle of the night. I took the time to employ these bonding opportunities even when I didn't feel like it. In almost every case, I was rewarded with a quiet, smiling daughter. In the cases that I was unsuccessful, my wife stepped in so I could go back to sleep.

Rewards

No matter your child's age, there are rewards to being a good parent. Trust me: we have a twenty-four-year-old and a five-week-old with four others in between. I've experienced many heart-warming plateaus with my children and I expect many more.

So in the overall scheme of things, the issue of a crying baby is minor. Just wait until your son uses his face for brakes one week after learning to ride a bicycle. As you lift him, screaming and bloody from the asphalt, this entire baby crying stuff will become minor. In fact, you don't really think of it at all unless you have another child. Once you watch your children grow and look back on their achievements and victories, their crying fades quickly into the recesses of your mind. The first couple months of endurance are well spent and rarely recalled.

It's OK to let her cry

Why do I keep dwelling on this subject? Because crying and stress are real issues. Forget reality television. When your baby has enough to eat, is not in pain, has a clean diaper and still insists on screaming bloody murder—that's reality. You must be willing to let her cry herself to sleep. Sometimes you just have to do this. Amazingly, even though she sounds like she's in the throes of a violent death, she'll live through it. She'll tire of her efforts and fall asleep. This is a cue for you and Mom to follow suit. Recharge your batteries so that you can bond with your baby again. This is a big bonding tip: *Get as much rest as you can, when you can*, so that you'll be able to handle the demands a baby places on you and your household.

Hunger and your baby's cries

I've observed by raising four children from birth that when your baby gives you her "hunger" cry, it's not always best to act immediately.

Unlike the diaper situation, if you react right away your little baby may not eat much. Babies will cry at the slightest pang of hunger. They know that when the hunger pang strikes, it gets increasingly worse, so they immediately act on it. Often, they don't need to be fed at that moment. If they are, they tend to fall asleep before they eat anything of consequence.

Interact with your baby and interest her in a playful game. She may be distracted by the prospect of playtime with Dad and ignore her hunger pangs. After a while the hunger will grow to a more pronounced level. She'll cry sporadically. Let your baby demand to be fed, which she'll eventually do. If she gets a little worked up, she'll be more prone to stay awake during the feeding. As mentioned earlier, eating tends to put babies to sleep. We call this "knock-out drops." If you feed your child just before your favorite show or the big game, she'll most likely sleep through it all. This is another great opportunity for you to relieve Mom and bond with your baby.

Learn to mimic your baby

I mentioned earlier that I mimic Veronica's peacock cries. I think it's a good idea to mimic all the different sounds your child makes. You don't want to become connected to just her crying, as she may grow to associate you with crying. Babies make some of the coolest sounds you'll ever hear. Your baby's cooing and vocalizations are the beginnings of verbal communications. If you copy them well enough, your baby will stop and look intently at you. When you make eye contact, you know your child is aware of you.

Get "hold" of a restless baby

When your baby gets restless—and trust me, all babies will—it's a good idea to have previously practiced a number of different ways to hold her. The change of position will often pacify her, at least temporarily. This

gives you an opportunity to find other diversions or to get to a changing table or to Mom or whatever your baby needs at that moment.

There are many ways to hold your baby. Take the time to learn the different ways your baby likes to be held. You can cradle her in your right or left arm. You can put her up on your right shoulder or your left. You can hold her facing forward from your stomach or either side. You can hold her out away from you with your right hand behind her head and your left hand under her bottom or vice-versa. Some holds your baby will like and some she won't. Even the ones that appear to please her may, at times, not be the way she wants to be held, so you should experiment with as many different positions as possible. By doing this, you learn which ones to use when she's fussing loudly and a change of position is needed.

This act of trying different positions also helps your baby to develop trust in you and to bond with your touch. Hopefully you're talking to her as you do this. Remember to always take advantage of as many bonding techniques as are available at any given time.

In this chapter we covered stress, the different cries a baby has and how you can step in and handle the situation deftly. There are many fathers out there who won't step in and handle their children when the going gets tough. I've been amazed at how the investment of my time, especially in moments of stress, has opened doors with my children that many fathers never know.

In basketball, players dream of being the "go-to" guy. I'm here to tell you that you can be the "go-to" guy with your children if you just take fatherhood seriously and step in when your children need you. Do they need you when all is going well? Oh yes, most definitely. They always want to share their victories.

But what about when the chips are down? Are you going to be there? Will you step up and be the comforter, the rescuer—the father. Develop a rapport with your baby when she's unhappy. That teenager that looms on the horizon needs you as much as the baby in your arms. Realize that what you do now establishes the base for what you do then. You can build a strong bond that will help your baby through those very tough teenage years. I know you can do it because I've done it.

Chapter 11: Reading to Your Baby

Now I want to introduce one of the simplest, easiest and potentially most enjoyable opportunities to bond with your baby. Would you have thought of reading and talking as "bonding with your baby?" While I may have arrived at that conclusion eventually, this did not top the list of bonding tips when I began developing this book. It makes perfect sense now. I love to read, so when I discovered this bonding tip, I was ecstatic.

Talking or speaking was a way to bond that I *had* considered when I began to write this book. The reasons why you should do this are fascinating. Not only *should* you talk to your baby, you *need* to speak to her in order to give her the best possible start in life.

An important fact in relation to mimicking your child's vocalizations: by the end of their second month of life, babies actively seek stimuli. I'm convinced dads are some of the best stimuli a baby can have. But you must be involved. It's important to be in contact with your baby, that she be familiar with your touch, your voice, your skin, etc. This is all preparation for the fun times ahead.

Why you should read to your baby

Studies have shown language skills and even intelligence are related to how many words an infant hears each day.

Here's something to do with your voice. Reading out loud is both preparation for school and a tremendous bonding opportunity. I like to read science fiction. You might laugh at the prospect of reading Isaac Asimov to your baby, but actually it's a good idea.

Reading also provides a great opportunity for cuddling. For an infant, the rhythm of the language is more important than the content. So pull out the old comic books or the sports page or anything *you* enjoy reading – *Green Eggs and Ham*® will come soon enough. Read what *you* like and expose your baby to the many different words and rhythms of our language. Reading to her gives her a leg up on future skills in life. Also, by reading aloud, your own comprehension level will rise dramatically so you can tackle that tough reading you have been putting off.

On February 15, 2006, the editorial page of the *Charleston Gazette* (Charleston, West Virginia), carried this short article:

> *West Virginia Kids Count Fund surveyed 608 adults in Kanawha, Lincoln, Mason, Putnam and Roane counties and came up with some interesting results.*
>
> *Ninety-nine percent of the adults agreed that showing affection to small children is important in their learning to read. Likewise, 97 percent identified reading to children as important, while 89 percent correctly identified rhyming or singing with children, 88 percent identified talking to children, and 83 percent identified playing with children. These adults seemed to recognize instinctively what research has shown – that all these activities contribute to a developing brain and help children learn to read.*
>
> *What adults did not instinctively know is when these activities should begin. Most people thought adults should begin preparing a child to read at age three. Only 15 percent said age one. Among low-income people and those with a high school education or less, only ten percent said age one.* **Yet the answer is that preparing children to read should begin at birth.** (Emphasis mine).

I find that very interesting. I want my children to have the best start to life that I can provide. I want to give them the absolute best chance for success at reading. Therefore I started incorporating the activities mentioned in this article *from birth*. Unfortunately this type of information did not make it into my life, either from home, through school or any other avenue of experience, until I began researching this book. No one told me anything like this. The article goes on:

> *... their brains are growing and developing even before they are born. Old-fashioned activities, such as singing to babies, playing rhyming games, reading to them and identifying and naming objects, stimulates developing brains. Those activities help babies to acquire language and patterns they will need later on.*

I'm writing this book for twenty-first century men. We know what it is like in the "real world" and we've come to understand how critical reading and language skills are. These basics are the tools our children will need to be successful in life. This is an opportunity for us as fathers to give our children a boost into life that we may otherwise let slip away through ignorance. Singing, rhyming games, naming objects, etc., appear so simple that any child could do it. But someone needs to show them how. *We*, as fathers, should show them how.

Talking to your baby

I constantly talk to Veronica. If I'm holding her, I'm verbalizing. Sometimes I imagine her thinking, "Shut up already, Dad, you're driving me over the edge!" Speaking to your baby is just a natural thing to do. Watch what happens anytime someone walks up to admire your little one. The first thing they do is talk to her! And some of the voices they use are quite creative.

Remember to ask questions when you're talking to your child in the early months of her life. Let her hear what a question sounds like, even if she can't understand the words. I think it's a natural response hard-wired into humans to know that language is critical to the development of children. Even though she can't speak, the rhythm of language is important for later communication skills, so why not expose your baby to all types of language?

By all types of language, I mean questions, exclamations, whispers, shouts of joy—basically all the various inflections, intonations and textures our language contains. All these are means to emphasize ideas and feelings and understanding. We want to give our children these critical tools. The really cool thing about this is the tremendous bonding opportunity reading and speaking lend you as a father.

I ask you, could there be any simpler way to bond with your baby? Speaking comes naturally to us as humans. Even if we don't talk much in public, speech is something we can easily incorporate into our interaction with our babies. This actually holds true for the rest of your life. By developing these reading and speaking times with your baby from birth (or before), you're developing a relationship (a bond) that will carry you through the rest of your life with this child.

> *Many people like to read or sing to their babies while they are still in the womb.*

Reading is something we all need to do more. By reading, you enhance your own intelligence and knowledge, even if it's in relation to *The Green Lantern* and *Spiderman*. Reading increases vocabulary. A good vocabulary allows you to express yourself better. By improving your ability to express yourself, when you come into the rough waters of those teenage years (hard to imagine while holding that little one, isn't it?), you'll be better equipped to guide your child through them into adulthood.

Just think, all those side benefits, and you form a strong bond to boot. Read to your baby. Talk to her all the time. Develop and nurture that bond. If you do, your own future self will be grateful and so will your child's.

Chapter 12: Family

When your entire family is involved in bonding with your newborn, many good things come of it. The process establishes a support group that your child will be able to rely on in later years. It gives your child a sense of security. The involvement of the whole family can smooth out tough times because there are more people helping. There can be a few hiccups as well, but that's true in every situation in our lives. Get your family involved in bonding with your baby. A dad can be a strong voice to advocate the involvement of others, especially when he himself is involved.

Importance of whole family bonding

One of the best things any family can do is to join together in a tight family bond. Using bonding techniques together with Mom and any older children in the house will communicate a strong familial message to your baby. Babies soak up all the input the world can give them. They learn things at incredible speeds. The added stimuli of Mom, Dad and siblings will help your baby see and feel ties that go beyond one-on-one.

Teaching other children in the family to consistently interact with their new sibling should be a priority. Make sure younger family members are supervised, but by all means teach them some of the bonding tips presented in this book. As they become more comfortable and connected to their sibling, and as your baby grows with them, these bonds will pay off for everyone concerned. Your older children will learn how to take care of their baby sibling (depending on their age), allowing you and Mom some rest or one-on-one time. Your little one will come to know she can count on her siblings for support.

Parents need a break every now and then

Older children are an excellent opportunity for parents to get a break from the daily demands of an infant. If you don't have older children, hire a babysitter. Mom definitely needs a break now and then and she needs adult conversation and company. After a while, all the baby talk, crying, diapers, feedings and everything else can cause an emotional meltdown. These meltdowns may even come faster for dad when *he's* the one providing constant care for the baby. Since fathers typically don't fill this role, it can be even more wearing on them.

Treat yourselves to a much-needed break and go out. If you're on a tight budget, stroll through the park or make a bag lunch and eat at a lake or some other serene locale. Be each other's saviors. Your baby will benefit from two people ready to meet her needs when you return.

The value of teamwork

By including everyone in the family in the raising of your baby, you effectively reduce jealousy and form a tighter family unit that teams up to help out in the care of its littlest member. But this can't be a one-shot deal. Only time and consistent exposure to siblings will build strong bonds.

Families play games

When my daughter, Ivy, was eleven months old, my wife and I went on a cruise to the Bahamas. We left Ivy with Bobbie's parents. We were only gone four days, but it was a refreshing time for the two of us, and Ivy had quite a good time herself.

When we returned to Florida, Grandpa showed us a fun little game he liked to play with his granddaughter. He would place a hand towel over his head and call out, "Where's Ivy? Where did she go? I can't find her! Ivy, where are you?"

Ivy would pull the towel from his head and proceed to howl with laughter. Just watching the two of them was entertaining enough, but the incident showed me that infants can have a grand time with the simplest of games. They love things that apparently make no sense to them, like the bubbles and balloons I mentioned earlier. Grandpa not knowing she was right there in front of him was one of those nonsensical games that delighted Ivy.

Milestones should be shared

Ivy also took her very first steps while we were on that vacation, which is another reason to stay connected to your new baby. These milestones of growth pass by quickly. Blink and you'll miss some of the most gratifying feelings a parent can know.

My son, Nicholas, walked at eight months while Bobbie and I were on a one-on-one vacation with him in tow. Ok, so it wasn't quite a one-on-one, but little Nick was more pleasure than bother. I vividly remember the day we sat on the floor and he walked from Bobbie to me and back. Nine years later this episode is still fresh in my mind. Thinking back, I'm not sure exactly where we stayed on that vacation or what we did, but I clearly remember sitting on the floor with Nick walking between the two of us. He was quite pleased with himself too.

Bobbie and I both remember the day he walked and our excitement at how early this happened in his little life. By sharing this moment we have a very special memory that enlivens us when we talk about it with others. Nick doesn't mind hearing that he walked earlier than his siblings either.

The politics of extended family

The subject of relatives brings me to a point of political delicacy. We all have well-meaning relatives. You know, – an aunt who wants to "give the parents a break," or grandmothers who want to show you how to handle your baby. I'm not by any means knocking these wonderful people. However, these well-meaning folks may intrude upon your bonding opportunities with your baby. Politely stand your ground. Give them their time with her, but remember, time alone with your baby is invaluable. Both you and your baby need it to deepen that bond.

Be the one who steps in

I've already talked about the importance of staying calm in stressful situations and of stepping in to take control when your baby is hungry or needs a diaper changed or is just fussy. One more great reason to do all those things is that, when you do, you're leading your family by example.

Don't wait for your wife or grandma to handle the mess. Send a message that you're an active, involved father. This is the prescription to take the edge off when your little baby is crying and tensions are building. Seeing Dad calm and in control will encourage teamwork from other children or extended family. They will be more willing to follow suit, and may tackle those dirty diapers themselves without prompting. Your mother-in-law will be impressed as well.

I'm not advocating you deny in-laws, uncles and grandparents time with your baby. I'm saying that these relatives can be intrusive and you'll miss some very important bonding time if you're not careful. This is not rocket science. The more time spent with your baby, the stronger the bond. It's that simple. Let your extended family have its fair share of time, but don't let yourself be muscled out of yours simply because you're a dad. Your baby needs you.

The value of help

In my house right now, in addition to Veronica, I have three children, ages twelve, ten and seven. Often, when Veronica begins to cry, there's a mad dash to see who can calm her. Her siblings also do this in the car, which is most appreciated by both parents. The pay-off for the little one is that she's treated more lovingly, even though she's the source of stress on those around her.

In order for the other children's efforts to work, it's important that your emotions stay tuned to not only your baby, but to others in the house as well. If any of the older children are having a bad day, you don't want them to take their frustrations out on their littlest sibling. While older children can be a huge help, they also don't necessarily have the patience to deal with a cranky baby. Recognize the importance of monitoring the family and of having willing hands to step in and help.

Learn to discern

You can also try to pick up on your baby's emotions as she presents them. The only way to accomplish this is to be present and observant. Your baby won't be talking for a while, but you can pick up on when she's in a contemplative mood (quiet and observing everything around her), or adventurous (straining to turn herself over).

While physical acts themselves are obvious, each one has an emotion attached to it which may require more careful observation to figure out. Does your baby look with wide-eyed wonderment at the world around her? Does she get frustrated when she's attempting to roll over? Does she quietly persevere? Point out to relatives and immediate family members each little nuance you observe. Share with them the thrill of your baby and you'll tie the bond of family tightly around your wonderful little son or daughter.

When all is said and done, the stronger the family bond, the better off your baby will be in later years. As I write these statements they appear to be self-evident. But if they're truly so apparent, why don't more families take the time to bond and be close? One reason is that fathers typically don't get involved until age three and up. By then patterns are already in place that make bonding more difficult—patterns like Mom handling all the childcare duties, other siblings following Dad's lead and not wanting to be involved, extended family members inwardly shaking their heads at the family dynamic displayed before them even though their own immediate family was probably no better.

Fathers play a critical role when it comes to family bonding. When a father *is* involved, others take note. Other siblings are *very* aware of this and are more easily sold on the idea of bonding with their little sister or brother. Extended family members are pleasantly surprised and want to join in on the camaraderie as well. Because many fathers have been distant from their newborns over the preceding generations, a father who encourages bonding throughout the family stands out as a leader. This enables him to accomplish the much cherished, and all too rare, full family bond. Take the lead. Bond with your baby and encourage immediate and extended family members to do the same.

Chapter 13: Be Prepared for Challenges

When we think about stress we realize it's everywhere. I don't believe there's a human on earth who doesn't experience stress. It's how we handle stress that defines us. As fathers, we should be leaders. We should stand strong and invest our time bonding with our baby. So what do we do when the stress overwhelms us?

It's going to happen. There will be a day and time when you're not quite able to take on your little one. I encourage you to take my suggestions in the paragraphs that follow as well as develop systems of your own. How we handle stress while interacting with our newborns determines how we'll bond with them. This is a critical time, a time to take stock of yourself and come out of the situation strong and feeling love for your child.

How to handle frustration

Frustration. It happens to all dads. It happens to all moms. Heck, it happens to everyone. But when the frustration centers around your baby, you need to pause and take stock of yourself. This is a "moment of truth" time in life in which you need to employ a level head. Babies pick up on agitation, frustration and anger. At times, when you're overly emotional, you may need to step away from the situation and your baby, and collect yourself.

Do whatever it takes for you to refocus and realize the tiny little life screaming at you needs her father to react in a loving and controlled manner. Babies only cry for a few reasons: pain, hunger, messy diaper or attention. Run this list through your head while you're calming down, and pinpoint her need. If you're driving and her screams are getting to you, pull over, get out, walk around and calm down. If you're running late, be late. I say this because bad things happen when we get overstressed. We tend to make bad decisions.

Some basic calming methods

- ✓ Method one: Step away from the situation.
- ✓ Method two: Seek help.
- ✓ Method three: Seek advice.
- ✓ Method four: Analyze the situation rather than react.

Step away from stress, anger and frustration when dealing with your baby. A level head is an important trait to model to your children at any age.

When your newborn is stressing you out and you've stepped away for a moment, sometimes you still feel overwhelmed. Seek out help. Find Mom, a sibling, an extended family member or a friend. It's much easier to cope with a frustrating episode when you involve someone else.

There are two things to keep in mind about asking for help. One – This does not scream to everyone who sees it that you're weak or incompetent. On the contrary, the fact that you recognize you need assistance and actually ask for it shows strength and leadership qualities. Too often we get caught up in the erroneous belief that asking for help is something bad. I'm here to tell you that it's one of the strongest and wisest decisions you can make. Two – by asking for help from family members, whether they're immediate or extended, you're actively building a familial bond between you, them and your baby. This is a good thing. This develops family ties that your little one will have for the rest of her life.

Another important stress management tip is to seek advice from Mom. Not *your* mother (although she could be of some help as well), but the mother of your baby. Prepare for this situation in advance by asking that Mom let you soothe the baby whenever she cries and feed her as often as possible. Rather than Mom running to the rescue all the time, you step in and practice doing what needs to be done to solve the problem. You'll be better equipped to handle your stress by learning ways to make your baby calm.

Eighty percent of a mother's interaction with her baby is triggered by crying. The significance of this is far-reaching, but in terms of your fatherhood, it means you have a ready-made role to fill—a relief pitcher for Mom. Because we dads tend to be more spontaneous, agitating (in a good way), and physical in our interactions with our children we give them a fresh perspective on parental reaction to crying. This is a tremendous opportunity to capitalize on the differences between a mom and a dad.

Moms fill a necessary role in a baby's life just as dads do. In fact, both roles are crucial. Mom can give you valuable insight into how she deals with a crying baby and you can then decide on a plan of how you handle the same situation. Dads need to balance the caregiving role to positively influence their children for the rest of their lives. Take advantage of the opportunity before you. Mom will be most grateful for your interest in her methods because raising a baby is a twenty-four-hour-a-day adventure that is best shared and enjoyed together.

You can also manage your stress by approaching the situation analytically rather than reacting emotionally. Often, it's not your newborn that has you whacked out, but something at work or some unresolved conflict in your life. Don't feel like the lone stranger. We all have varying forms of unresolved conflict. As fathers, we have an obligation to make sure we don't transmit this agitation in our lives to our babies. That's bad bonding. In fact, it's not bonding at all; it's the building of barriers to bonding. Fathers need to be aware of stress and not let it hinder the bonding process.

This past week, Veronica turned seven weeks old. She had just begun smiling a bit in week six, which surprised me since I thought I had a couple more weeks to go before I would be rewarded with such beauty. Last week, her smiling started to become more prevalent. She appears to enjoy seeing me smile, which triggers a smile from her. When I laugh out loud, her smile explodes in a face-devouring grin that melts my heart. Fathers live for these moments; they're a reward for all the work and effort and sacrifice you put into raising your baby and bonding with her.

When Veronica smiles at me, or Nick comes up and hugs me, or Ivy insists on a kiss, or Allie cuddles up on my lap, all the diapers, frustrations and challenges are forgotten. Enjoy the role you have ready-made for you as a father. Savor those special times as they arrive so that the next time you're challenged by the endless crying, you know something awesome is coming your way if you just remain calm and take the time to bond with your baby.

If I had to point to one bonding tip that impacts your children in a conscious, meaningful way, it's how you handle stress. When you're under fire, when life is giving you all you can manage, your ability to step back, take stock and move forward teaches children of all ages, from newborn on up, how to handle what life throws at them. This is a critical bond that you need to build. When you calmly handle stressful times with your baby, you teach her that she can do the same

Chapter 14: Rewards of Bonding

There are wonderful times, events and memories on the horizon for you and your child. This tiny little baby will one day ask your approval for her mate or ask for the keys to your car or simply walk up out of the blue and give you a hug. You can't begin to imagine what potential your child has to impact your life and this world.

There will come a time when you'll wish you could show your adult child what she was like when she was just beginning to explore life. I will give some suggestions in this chapter for ways and means to accomplish this task. Use these methods to develop your own ways to preserve what is special about and to your baby now, so that she can enjoy the memories later.

Prepare for future dividends of bonding

Everyone enjoys recounting the special times, places and people that made up their childhood. I'm forty-eight years old and this is as true of me as it is of people I've met throughout my life. With this in mind, endear yourself to your child when she's older, possibly even an adult, by employing a calendar and a pen now. Use the calendar as a daily journal.

Also, consider writing a blog that recounts special moments from her life that you, as a father, cherish. Write short snippets of what your baby is doing, how you're feeling or significant occurrences in the growth of your child. Stash these calendars in a box large enough to store a few years' worth. Put them in a special place so they won't be lost or damaged. It may be a couple decades before you pull them out and share them.

There will come a day when both of you will want to reminisce. This could be a tool your child will remember and one day use while she's bonding with *her* newborn.

Keepsakes

In addition, save keepsake items like a special blanket or a favorite toy. In the case of either, buy a duplicate (if possible) so that if the original is damaged you'll still have something viable to present to your grown child.

Playthings around the house that connect

Speaking of toys, if you're looking for something for your six-month-old to play with, household objects like plastic bowls and cups can often be more entertaining than toys. I believe one reason for this is that they see their parents using them and they want to be like Mom and Dad. It's amazing the playtime your baby can get from pots and pans. This sometimes makes me feel foolish for buying some expensive toy that my daughter will not even look at. If you can get some good video of her rockin' the pots and pans like a drum set, everyone will get a kick out of it when she's all grown up.

Other fathers

Do you know any other men with infant children? Schedule a regular get-together of just the fathers and their children for some play time. Remember, your baby needs your attention, so this is *baby's night out*, not Dad's. This can be an opportunity to get feedback from other dads on what they're doing that works with their children. It can also be an opportunity to commiserate over common unsuccessful efforts.

You can coordinate with the other dads on trips to specific places. Any time you can take your baby out somewhere—for a ride, to the store, the mall, the zoo, etc.—do it. The stimulus of these different places exposes your baby to the wide, wonderful world. Also, she will associate you with new and exciting things. By sharing this experience with other fathers, you can develop a strong support group that is comfortable together.

Each father can point out various aspects of his surroundings. Just think of the varying smells of the places mentioned above. Your car has a familiar (specific), smell. In a deli, someone may be baking bread or frying up lunch. The produce section of the grocery store usually has a variety of appealing scents. The mall's food court may be an obvious choice in regard to smells, but department stores also have a variety of aromas. The candle section, the perfume section, the shoe department and the clothes themselves offer new olfactory experiences for your baby. It is good for your child to observe other fathers involved with their children, just like you are with her.

Dads and their babies in public

There's a somewhat unnerving aspect of being a dad out alone with a newborn: women just walk up to you and start talking to you, asking questions about your baby. They always come smiling and friendly. This is just another indication of how special a baby is. I have found I feel a sense of pride when women are visibly surprised by how involved I am with my baby.

Journaling your baby's early life

Did you know that your baby's eye color is not necessarily set until months after birth? Changing eye color is very interesting. My wife is full-blooded Greek and I have English and Irish ancestry. One of my sisters has two redheads. So far I have two brunettes and one strawberry blonde, but no blue eyes in my children. Veronica still has blue eyes, so I check often to see if there's any shift in color. This brings on many a staring contest, which is extremely gratifying. When your little baby locks eyes with you, all the warmth a relationship can hold will wash over you.

By listing examples like these and many others, your baby can grow up and read your thoughts and stories about her at an age she can't remember. So much is forgotten over the years by both the father and the child. By recording special moments and observations, no matter how small, you preserve those special times for both of you.

Other physical triumphs and milestones

Teach your baby that she has hands and can do things with them. You'll most likely have to pry open her fingers, as most babies keep their fists balled up a lot. Place a rattle in her hand. Sounds are fun for children, and when they can make them on their own it's even more entertaining.

Other milestone developments include smiling, rolling over unassisted, crawling, walking and talking. Your baby should begin smiling (other than for passed gas) around the two-month mark. I always look forward to this time as I love to make my children laugh. Actually, I believe most dads are like that. It's one of the great payoffs to being an involved father. When your baby spies you and her face lights up in a totally unabashed smile, you know the bond of fatherhood. This is as thrilling as anything you'll experience in life.

Rolling over may not sound like a big deal, but your baby is coordinating motor functions when she accomplishes this feat. Crawling is not far behind, and then a whole new era of activity springs upon you. You get used to your child's immobility, then all of a sudden you have to baby-proof your house. Hopefully you realized this when she was born and you won't have to run around one day baby-proofing out of desperation. Yes, it has happened to me.

You do realize, of course, that your newborn baby is going to grow up. That might seem like a silly statement of obvious fact, but I mention it for a reason. All too often, we don't keep that thought in mind when we're deciding to go play a round of golf or work late or anything else that keeps us from spending time with our baby.

A favorite TV show, or the desire to get a little extra sleep, is a convenient excuse for not interacting with our little ones. One of the points I hope I made in this chapter is that what we get in the future far outweighs some mindless television show, bad golf score or that report that was so vitally important to have finished by 8:00 a.m. Monday. Twenty years from now, you'll realize that report has fallen into the wasteland of forgotten human endeavor.

In that same scenario, an hour spent each day with your baby as she grows gives you something tangible, real and satisfying twenty years later, or forty for that matter. Look to reap the rewards of fatherhood by bonding with your baby now. Every minute is another opportunity. Seize the moment.

Chapter 15: Building a Legacy

As a father, are you building your legacy for yourself, or are you building it for your children? The answer is yes and yes. You're also building it for your grandchildren, nieces, nephews and any other family member who sees your bond grow with your child throughout her life. You should also think of it as something seen by your friends and acquaintances.

The fact is that you can't escape your legacy as a father. As I mention later in this chapter, you build one from the moment of conception. Like it or not, this is an inescapable fact. I say, cherish it. Defend your legacy. Pass on to your baby something she can cherish and pass on to her children. In this final chapter let's explore how to do just that.

Work daily toward your legacy

Building a strong legacy as a loving father takes a daily effort. You should find ways to interact with your baby every day. The main purpose of this book is to help direct you in various ways to accomplish that. Why daily? We all learn through repetition. From our earliest moments of life, repetition is a key component in our discovery of our world and the way it works. Consistent daily exposure to Dad is something your baby not only needs, but also desires. When you give that attention to your baby, the benefits are far-reaching and immeasurable.

Each child develops her own set of attributes that makes her a unique individual. As you watch your baby grow and take on new personality traits, you can't help but be drawn to her and anticipate who she'll become next. The layers of personality that determine who your baby will eventually become are being built at the earliest ages.

A legacy is for life

By building your legacy daily, you'll make it stick for a lifetime. Your baby will carry memories of your interactions with her all of her life. The father who's intricately involved with his baby on a daily basis will be a beloved father who passes on many good traits. That is a legacy to aspire to, to strive for and to pursue. This legacy is easily attainable through the daily sacrifice of time spent doing something you'll always cherish.

I interviewed many fathers who shared fond stories of bonding with their newborns. The most mentioned bonding event, and obviously a favorite, was the experience of letting their babies fall asleep on their chests. One father related how pillows were quickly tossed around his easy chair whenever he sat down with his baby. The pillows were a precaution against the baby falling off, in the event Dad also fell asleep. (Which never happened, but it was a thoughtful precaution.)

> *I met an older gentleman who told me to videotape my two-year-old because the personality I see there will be her defining personality when she enters her twenties. I found that an interesting concept. I will be paying close attention to whether that holds true, but regardless, personality and temperament are developed very early in life.*

A legacy is forged by a bond

I have personally enjoyed the closeness and trust my children have placed in me by falling asleep on my chest. Despite being twelve, ten and seven, they still crawl into my chair with me and curl up for a movie. You can't easily develop this kind of bond after they begin walking and talking. If you've been distant up to that point, your child will be wary of such a display of trust and affection.

I like the way one gentleman I talked with describes his chest-sleeping son:

> *"It seems that my son and I bonded from the very beginning. My fondest memories of him as a baby are when he cried for whatever reason, and I lay down with him on my chest. This calmed him immediately, and was very comforting to me as well. He became so accustomed to this that as he got older and was crawling around, he would catch me napping on the couch and would climb up and lie on my chest and "talk" to me. To this day we have a strong bond that can never be broken."*

> *H.B., St. Albans, WV*

This is exactly the type of legacy a father looks forward to with his children. When you spend that extra little time with your child to forge a bond, the effects are felt for a lifetime. And if you successfully pass on your legacy of a strong bond to your children, the effects of thirty minutes here, an hour there, will stretch across your lifetime, your child's and on to successive generations.

Every father builds a legacy

The American Heritage Dictionary defines legacy as "something handed down from an ancestor or predecessor." So, every father hands down his bonding legacy whether he likes it or not.

My own father doesn't care for his legacy. He's apologized on numerous occasions for his lack of attention during my youth. I was his only son (he also has three daughters) and he spent precious little time with me one-on-one.

The emotional distance between us reflects that. Only through great effort and a lot of forgiveness have we been able to forge a bond as adults, although it's nowhere near what it could have been. This is a critical mistake no one sets out to make, but it happens all too often. I love my father. I love his strengths, his ability to weave creative stories, his strong work ethic and his sense of what makes people laugh.

I would love to go back and try again, to see how different life would be if we had connected from my birth. That, of course, is not possible. I cherish the relationship we currently have and I'm determined to learn from our mistakes. I strive to interact with my children on a daily basis. Sometimes I fail. The important thing is to recognize when we aren't taking the time to bond, and correct the situation.

When all is said and done here, what am I talking about, time-wise? Really, it boils down to thirty minutes here, an hour there, *but on a daily basis*. You can find the time for these precious moments. I also know that if you do, you'll discover few, if any, more compelling uses for your time than bonding with your baby.

Forge the legacy of a father revered and cherished by his children. Your legacy is born with your baby and built minute by minute, day by day. You can do this and you'll be glad you did.

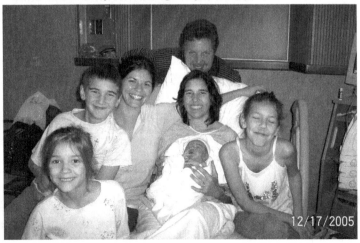

Glossary

auditory – relating to the process of hearing.

baby massage – rubbing or kneading the muscles of a baby as an aid to relaxation and bonding.

bonding – the formation of a close emotional tie between people.

caricature – a drawing, description, or performance that exaggerates somebody's characteristics for humorous or satirical effect.

conception – the fertilization of an egg by a sperm at the beginning of pregnancy.

day care – daytime supervision and recreational facilities for preschool children.

embryo – a human offspring in the early stages following conception up to the end of the eighth week, after which it is classified as a fetus.

expressed milk – the product of forcing milk from a mother's breast by squeezing.

father – 1. a man who is the parent of a human being. 2. a man who brings up and looks after a child as if he were the father.

fetus – an unborn baby at a stage when all the structural features of the adult are recognizable, usually after eight weeks of development.

journal – somebody's written daily record of personal experiences.

Lamaze – a method of natural childbirth by which a woman is physically and psychologically prepared through prenatal training. Lamaze encourages the use of controlled breathing and the participation of the woman's partner during the process of childbirth.

legacy – something that is handed down from a previous generation.

newborn – a baby. A newborn child.

new father – a father who's mate has just given birth whether the child is his first or tenth.

OB/Gyn – an obstetrician-gynecologist who assists in the birth of your baby.

onesie – an article of clothing for babies that has snaps between the legs for easy diaper changes. Looks like an adult woman's body suit.

pelvic cavity – the area in the abdominal area of women where the uterus forms during pregnancy.

personality – the totality of somebody's attitudes, interests, behavioral patterns, emotional responses, social roles, and other individual traits that endure over long periods of time.

placenta – a vascular (fluid carrying) organ that develops inside the uterus of most pregnant mammals to supply food and oxygen to the fetus through the umbilical cord. It is expelled after birth.

receiving blanket – a light blanket in which an infant is wrapped, especially after a bath.

role model – a worthy person; someone who is a good example for other people.

scenario – an imagined sequence of events, or an imagined set of circumstances.

sibling – a brother or sister.

sleep debt – the lack of sleep. Sleep deprivation. Feeling tired all the time due to lack of sleep.

smorgasbord – a wide variety.

Snugli® - a cloth device that straps a baby to the body of an adult, most often with the baby strapped to the adult's chest.

Sonogram – a graphical representation of sound, especially in the three dimensions of frequency, time, and intensity that produces a picture much like an x-ray but without radiation.

trimester – a period of three months, especially one of the three three-month periods into which human pregnancy is divided for medical purposes.

umbilical cord – the flexible, often spirally twisted tube that connects the abdomen of a fetus to the mother's placenta in the womb, and through which nutrients are delivered and waste expelled. Once born, the umbilical cord is cut, tied off, and becomes what is commonly referred to as the belly button.

uterus – a hollow muscular organ in the pelvic cavity of female mammals, in which the embryo is nourished and develops before birth.

womb – 1. a uterus, especially a woman's.   2. a place where something is conceived and nurtured.

Resource Sites for Dads

Great article for dads from Penn State University -
www.betterkidcare.psu.edu/ToddlerTopics/2003Issue5.pdf

Good bonding tips for dads – *http://kidsdirect.net/PD/fathers/tips.htm*

Effects of a father's depression on newborns -
http://news.bbc.co.uk/2/hi/health/4122346.stm

Excellent article on how dads contribute to breastfeeding - *http://www.dy-dee.com/html/breastfeeding_fathers.html*

A "Tips for Dad" article - *http://www.fathersworld.com/guest/tips.html*

More tips - *http://www.pregnancy-calendars.net/fathers-bonding.aspx*

Who determines birth weight of baby, father or mother? -
http://news.bbc.co.uk/2/hi/health/6154220.stm

American Academy of Pediatrics article on fathers -
http://www.aap.org/publiced/BK0_Fathers.htm

Excellent information and links for African American fathers supporting breastfeeding -
http://www.fns.usda.gov/wic/Fathers/SupportingBreastfeeding.HTM

University of Minnesota article on the importance of fathers to babies -
http://www.extension.umn.edu/info-u/babies/BE894.html

Great article, Fathers are Pregnant Too! -
http://www.labouroflove.org/conception-&-pregnancy/fathers-&-pregnancy/the-father-is-pregnant-too!/

Excellent tips presented in a list format -
http://world.std.com/~reinhold/babytips.html

Web MD article on the positive effect dad has in soothing fussy newborns
– *http://www.webmd.com/parenting/news/20070607/fathers-touch-soothes-newborns*

Great article from About.com on how to bond with your newborn -
http://fatherhood.about.com/od/newdadsresources/a/dad_bonding.htm

Male responsibility statistics in relation to teen pregnancies -
http://www.dhs.ca.gov/pcfh/prp/male/facts.html

Scientific analysis of why babies look like their fathers and the evolution of self deception -
http://www.psy.unipd.it/~pbressan/papers/why_babies.pdf

Fascinating article on the switch from childbirth in the home to hospitals -
http://www.birthpsychology.com/birthscene/index.html

Positive article on fathers of preemie babies who may or do die -
http://www.preemie-l.org/stimpson.html

Good article on fathers from ParentsDirect.com -
http://kidsdirect.net/PD/fathers/factor.htm

Study results on baby birth size due to diabetic fathers -
http://www.theage.com.au/articles/2003/01/05/1041566310356.html

Another good article on a father's role in breastfeeding -
http://life.familyeducation.com/nursing/fathers/35919.html

Does breastfeeding make your child smarter? From Stanford University - *http://www.stanford.edu/~rmahony/Breastfeeding.html*

Critical study on the effects of absentee fathers on their children - *http://www.fathersforlife.org/divorce/chldrndiv.htm*

Tips on dealing with a crying baby written to fathers - *http://www.childwelfare.gov/pubs/usermanuals/fatherhood/append_e_3.cfm*

Fatherhood blues after childbirth as related to sex and bonding with related information on sex before and after childbirth - *http://www.smh.com.au/articles/2002/12/11/1039379884341.html*

Brief description and contact information for Boot Camp for New Dads - *http://www.childwelfare.gov/pubs/usermanuals/fatherhood/chaptereight_a.cfm*

Nice blog on the topic of The Effects of Babies on Single Men - *http://www.visionforum.com/hottopics/blogs/dwp/2007/01/2031.aspx*

Another article on the importance of fathers in relation to their children - *http://parenting.amuchbetterway.com/2007/10/importance-of-fathers.html*

Extensive book (448 pages) on *Why Fathers Count* - *http://www.whyfatherscount.com/*

Incredibly well stocked page of links to everything father - *http://extension.missouri.edu/parentlink/Library/fathers.htm*

Excellent source of information for topics relating to family - www.tesh.com click on "inside tesh.com," then "Kids/Family"

Website for Signing DVD's – www.criticalthinking.com and type sign language in search box.

Ordering Information

Ways to Order *Fatherhood 101: Bonding Tips for Building Loving Relationships*

Visit the author's website at:
www.fatherhood-101.com

Visit the publisher's website at:
www.clearviewpress.net

Order by Phone at 1-386-290-7440

Order by Mail:
Send check or money order to ClearView Press, Inc.
    PO Box 353431, Palm Coast, FL 32135-3431
(Ten day wait for check processing before shipping.)

Other products available:

Booklet - 50 Bonding Tips for New Fathers,
Audio CD & Hardcover edition of Fatherhood 101
and more!

Michael Ray King grew up in a small town in West Virginia. The first twenty-two years of his life were spent in the lovely mountains of his home state. Upon graduation from college in 1981 he moved to Raleigh, North Carolina where he lived for the next seventeen years. It was in Raleigh that he met his wife Bobbie.

Michael and Bobbie have six children ranging from two years old to twenty-six as of the publication of this book. In 1998 Michael relocated his family to Florida and is now living in Palm Coast.

While basketball, bicycling and writing are some of his passions, it is his love of mountains that will someday carry him back. He shares a love of snow skiing with one of his daughters and plays basketball with his youngest son regularly. Bobbie and two of his daughters love horseback riding and one day the family aspires to have a rural home with horses, dogs and crackling fireplaces. Long walks on crisp autumn days are Michael's favorite times in life.

Michael is currently working on a book for the Joy & Care Giving Foundation, a non-profit organization that is building much needed schools and libraries in the Philippines. Helping children is high on his list of priorities. He coaches his youngest son's basketball team and continues to learn how to be the best father he can be.

He is available for speaking engagements and discussions on the topic of fatherhood. He can be contacted at:

author@michaelrayking.com

CPSIA information can be obtained at www.ICGtesting.com
Printed in the USA
LVOW01s1611080714

393405LV00011BA/104/P